BLOCKCHAIN TECHNOLOGY
BACICS

Blockchain, cryptography and cybersecurity

RAGHAVA SHANKAR

TABLE OF CONTENTS

The Blockchain innovation can be another name for the peruses however the specialists have a reliable assessment that because of this innovation we can observe a significant changeover in the field of change. Along these lines, different organizations are looking for right open doors in the area of Blockchain Application Development. The blockchain is a developing innovation so that, the vast majority of the general population don't know about this new headway. On the off chance that you are one of the individuals who wish to have significant learning of the innovation, bear on perusing the data gave underneath.

Blockchain Developer Tools

- **Solc**

Solc is the Solidity Compiler (Solidity is the programming language to write code on the Ethereum chain).

- **Embark**

It is a developer framework for Ethereum dapps, so it allows you to easily develop and deploy dapps, or a server less html5 application that uses decentralized technologies.

- **Ether Scripter**

This is a tool that helps you writing the script (or code) of your smart contract.

- **Tierion**

It enables to create a verifiable database of any data or process on the bitcoin blockchain by offering developer tools & API to add data to the distributed ledger.

- **Coinbase's API**

Coinbase's APIs allow blockchain developers to easily build new bitcoin apps and integrate bitcoin into already existing applications.

- **Mist**

For Ethereum developer, you can use Mist not only to store Ether or send transactions but also to deploy smart contracts.

- **BaaS**

Microsoft Azure created the so-called BaaS, or Blockchain as a service, a useful tool for developers to build dapps in a safe and cheaper environment that supports several chains, including MultiChain, Eris, Storj, and Augur.

What do we mean by Blockchain?

Blockchain works like a computerized record in which exchanges are made with the utilization of Bitcoin or cryptographic forms of money. As per the Blockchain specialists, this innovation gives a safe approach to making or recording every one of the exchanges, understandings or contracts. Also, Blockchain is significant for everything that should have been checked and kept in a safe, advanced biological system.

From the underlying purpose of the start of the system, the database is shared between various clients that are incorporated to get to the data of the considerable number of exchanges. The aggregate size of the system differs as indicated by the name of clients that might be a few clients or it might be a gathering of many the clients.

What is the utilization of Blockchain Technology?

The specialists are endeavoring to utilize it for more than one destination and these days, the most obvious and unmistakable utilization of the Blockchain innovation is Bitcoin. Bitcoin has been helping the general population occupied with budgetary exchanges since 2008. Furthermore, the specialists are looking for the courses by which a similar innovation can be utilized to comprehend or lessen security, question or conviction issues.

How is it utilized?

A unique PC programming is utilized to make the blockchain consequently to share the data with the database on account of a crisp exchange. A blockchain contains hinders that are hashed or encoded bunches of transfers. Each code, with the hash of the square before it, connects the two and structures the chain that is a Blockchain. This procedure needs the approval of each square to guarantee the security of the general database.

For what reason do we require Blockchain Development?

As specified over, the Blockchain is attempting to make the innovation more valuable for the general population who need to keep up an undeniable record of exchanges. The Blockchain innovation gives extreme lucidity and straightforwardness and can be utilized as a compelling instrument against the instances of debasement.

With the assistance of the Blockchain innovation, every one of the exchanges occurs in a sheltered domain where every one of the points of interest is scrambled with the age of a novel exchange number and this number is recorded in the record as a placeholder. For this situation, not every one of the clients would have the capacity to see the subtle elements of the exchange. Be that as it may, the system will know about the trade. This procedure restrains any difference in misrepresentation because the individual with noxious plans must access each PC to roll out improvements in the database.

Because of the expanding significance of the Blockchain improvement, various people or associations are searching for a trusted and stable Blockchain Development Company.

It involves trust and security, and in this way, Infogrames Software Solution is prepared to give tasteful answers for various industry verticals.

CHAPTER ONE

AN INTRODUCTION TO BLOCKCHAIN

What is Nodes?

A node is a device on a blockchain network that is in essence the foundation of the technology, allowing it to function and survive. Nodes are distributed across a widespread network and carry out a variety of tasks. In this segment of the Academy we will examine the qualities of a node on a blockchain network.

A node can be any active electronic device, including a computer, phone or even a printer, as long as it is connected to the internet and as such has an IP address. The role of a node is to support the network by maintaining a copy of a blockchain and, in some cases, to process transactions. Nodes are often arranged in the structure of trees, known as binary trees. Each cryptocurrency has its own nodes, maintaining the transaction records of that particular token.

Nodes are the individual parts of the larger data structure that is a blockchain. As the owners of nodes willingly contribute their computing resources to store and validate transactions they have the chance to collect the transaction fees and earn a reward in the underlying cryptocurrency for doing so. This is known as mining or forging.

Processing these transactions can require large amounts of computing and processing power, meaning that the average computer's capabilities are inadequate. Generally, professional miners tend to invest in extremely powerful computing devices known as CPUs (central processing units) or GPUs (graphics processing units) in order to keep up with the demand for processing power that is required for them to validate transactions and as such earn the rewards that comes with doing so.

Encryption mode

Examples of Encrypt and decrypt text

```
// Nodejs encryption with CTR

var crypto = require('crypto'),
```

```javascript
    algorithm = 'aes-256-ctr',

    password = 'd6F3Efeq';


function encrypt(text){

  var cipher = crypto.createCipher(algorithm,password)

  var crypted = cipher.update(text,'utf8','hex')

  crypted += cipher.final('hex');

  return crypted;

}


function decrypt(text){

  var decipher =
crypto.createDecipher(algorithm,password)

  var dec = decipher.update(text,'hex','utf8')

  dec += decipher.final('utf8');

  return dec;

}


var hw = encrypt("hello world")
```

```javascript
// outputs hello world

console.log(decrypt(hw));
```

Encrypt and decrypt buffers

```javascript
var crypto = require('crypto'),
    algorithm = 'aes-256-ctr',
    password = 'd6F3Efeq';

function encrypt(buffer){
  var cipher = crypto.createCipher(algorithm,password)
  var crypted =
Buffer.concat([cipher.update(buffer),cipher.final()]);
  return crypted;
}

function decrypt(buffer){
```

```
  var decipher = crypto.createDecipher
(algorithm,password)

  var dec = Buffer.concat([decipher.update(buffer) ,
decipher.final()]);

  return dec;

}



var hw = encrypt(new Buffer("hello world", "utf8"))

// outputs hello world

console.log(decrypt(hw).toString('utf8'));
```

Encrypt and decrypt streams

```
// Nodejs encryption of buffers

var crypto = require('crypto'),

   algorithm = 'aes-256-ctr',

   password = 'd6F3Efeq';
```

```javascript
var fs = require ('fs');

var zlib = require ('zlib');


// input file
var r = fs.createReadStream('file.txt');
// zip content
var zip = zlib.createGzip();
// encrypt content
var encrypt = crypto.createCipher(algorithm, password);
// decrypt content
var decrypt = crypto.createDecipher (algorithm, password)
// unzip content
var unzip = zlib.createGunzip();
// write file
var w = fs.createWriteStream('file.out.txt');


// start pipe
```

```
r.pipe(zip).pipe(encrypt).pipe(decrypt).pipe(unzip).pipe(w)
;
```

Crypto-what?

If you've endeavored to plunge into this secretive thing
called blockchain, you'd be excused for withdrawing with
dismay at the sheer murkiness of the specialized language
that is regularly used to outline it. So before we get into
what digital money is and how blockchain innovation may
change the world, how about we examine what blockchain
is.

In the most straightforward terms, a blockchain is an
advanced record of exchanges, much the same as the
records we have been utilizing for a long time to record
deals and buys. The capacity of this excellent record is,
indeed, virtually indistinguishable to a shared history in
that it files charges and credits between individuals. That is
the central idea driving blockchain; the distinction is who
holds the record and who checks the exchanges.

That is a considerable measure of obligation, so it's essential that Rob feels he can confide in his bank else he would not hazard his cash with them. He needs to feel sure that the bank won't deceive him, won't lose his money, won't be victimized, and won't vanish medium-term. This requirement for trust has supported practically every significant conduct and feature of the stable fund industry, to the degree that notwithstanding when it was found that banks were being untrustworthy with our cash amid the money related emergency of 2008, the legislature (another middle person) safeguarded them out as opposed to hazard pulverizing the last pieces of trust by giving them a chance to crumble.

Blockchains work contrastingly in one critical regard: they are altogether decentralized. There is no focal clearing house like a bank, and there is no focal record held by one element. Instead, the document is circulated over a vast system of PCs, called hubs, every one of which contains a duplicate of the whole album on their hard drives. These hubs are associated with each other using a bit of programming called a distributed (P2P) customer, which synchronizes information over the system of centers and ensures that everyone has a similar form of the record at some random point in time.

At the point when another exchange is gone into a blockchain, it is first scrambled utilizing best in class cryptographic innovation. Once encoded, the dialogue is changed over to something many refer to as a square, which is fundamentally the term used for a scrambled gathering of new transactions. That square is then sent (or communicate) into the system of PC hubs, where the centers check it and, once confirmed, went on through the system with the goal that the square can be added to the finish of the record on everyone's PC, under the rundown of every single past square. This is known as the chain. Subsequently, the tech is alluded to as a blockchain.

Once affirmed and recorded into the record, the exchange can be finished. This is the way digital forms of money like Bitcoin work.

Responsibility and the expulsion of trust

What are the benefits of this framework over a managing an account or focal clearing framework? For what reason would Rob utilize Bitcoin rather than typical money?

The appropriate response is trust. As said previously, with the saving money framework it is essential that Rob confides in his bank to ensure his cash and handle it legitimately. To guarantee this occurs, large administrative structures exist to confirm the activities of the banks and assure they are fit for the reason. Governments at that point control the controllers, making a kind of layered arrangement of checks whose sole intention is to help avert missteps and terrible conduct. Associations like the Financial Services Authority exist precisely because banks can't be trusted individually.

What's more, banks as often as possible commit errors and make trouble, as we have seen too often. When you have a solitary wellspring of power, control has a tendency to get manhandled or abused. The trust connection among individuals and banks is clumsy and unstable: we don't generally confide in them, yet we don't feel there are many options.

Blockchain frameworks, then again, needn't bother with you to confide in them by any stretch of the imagination. The hubs confirm all exchanges (or squares) in a blockchain in the system before being added to the record, which implies there is no single purpose of disappointment and no single endorsement channel. If a programmer needed to mess with the album on a blockchain effectively, they would need to all the while hacking a vast number of PCs, which is relatively unimaginable. A programmer would likewise be practically unfit to cut a blockchain organize down, as, once more, they would have the capacity to close down each, and every PC in a system of PCs conveyed far and wide.

The encryption procedure itself is likewise a key factor. Blockchains like the Bitcoin one utilize intentionally troublesome methods for their confirmation strategy. On account of Bitcoin, squares are checked by hubs playing out a deliberately processor-and time-concentrated arrangement of figuring's, regularly as riddles or complex numerical issues, which imply that confirmation is neither moment nor open. Centers that do submit the asset to verification of squares are rewarded with an exchange charge and an abundance of recently stamped Bitcoins. This has the capacity of both boosting individuals to wind up hubs (since preparing squares like this requires PCs and a considerable measure of power), while additionally taking care of the way toward producing - or stamping - units of the money. This is alluded to as mining since it includes a lot of exertion (by a PC, for this situation) to deliver another item. It additionally implies that exchanges are checked by the freest way that could be available, freer than an administration managed association like the FSA.

This decentralized, vote based and very secure nature of blockchain implies that they can work without the requirement for control (they are automatic), government or another hazy go-between. They work since individuals don't confide in one another, as opposed to regardless of.

Let the hugeness of that sink in for some time, and the enthusiasm around blockchain begins to bode well.

Shrewd contracts

Where things get fascinating is the uses of blockchain past cryptographic forms of money like Bitcoin. Given that one of the basic standards of the blockchain framework is the safe, autonomous confirmation of exchange, it's anything but painful to envision different manners by which this kind of process can be profitable. Numerous such applications are as of now being used or advancement. A portion of the best ones are:

Brilliant contracts (Ethereum): likely the most energizing blockchain improvement after Bitcoin, savvy agreements are hindering that contain code that must be executed all together for the deal to be satisfied. The system can be anything, as long as a PC can run it, yet in basic terms, it implies that you can utilize blockchain innovation (with its independent confirmation, trustless design, and security) to make a sort of escrow framework for any exchange. For instance, in case you're a website specialist you could make an agreement that checks if another customer's site is propelled or not, and after that naturally, discharge the assets to you once it is. No all the more pursuing or invoicing. Keen contracts are additionally being utilized to demonstrate responsibility for the resource, for example, property or artistry. The potential for decreasing misrepresentation with this methodology is tremendous.

Distributed storage (Storj): distributed computing has reformed the web and achieved the coming of Big Data which has, like this, kick began the new AI insurgency. In any case, most cloud-constructed frameworks are kept running concerning servers put away in single-area server ranches, claimed by a single substance (Amazon, Rackspace, Google and so forth). This exhibits all the same issues from the managing an accounting framework, in that your information is controlled by a single, obscure association which speaks to a sole purpose of disappointment. Dispersing information on a blockchain evacuates the trust issue and furthermore guarantees to expand consistent quality as it is such a significant amount of harder to bring a blockchain to arrange down.

Advanced recognizable proof (Sheard): two of the most significant issues within the recent memory are separate burglary and information insurance. With huge brought together administrations, for example, Facebook holding such a substantial amount of information about us, and endeavors by different created world governments to store advanced data about their nationals in a local database, the potential for maltreatment of our knowledge is unnerving. Blockchain innovation offers a potential answer for this by wrapping your key information up into a scrambled square that can be checked by the blockchain arrange at whatever point you have to demonstrate your personality. The utilization of this range from the undeniable substitution of international IDs and I.D. cards to different regions, for example, supplanting passwords. It could be enormous.

Computerized voting: profoundly topical in the wake of the examination concerning Russia's impact on the ongoing U.S. decision, electronic voting has for quite some time been associated with being both problematic and exceedingly defenseless against altering. Blockchain innovation offers a method for checking that a voter's vote was effectively sent while holding their secrecy. It guarantees not exclusively to decrease misrepresentation in races yet additionally to expand overall voter turnout as individuals will have the capacity to vote on their cell phones.

Blockchain innovation is still particularly in its early stages, and a large portion of the applications are far from general utilize. Indeed, even Bitcoin, the most settled blockchain stage, is liable to colossal instability demonstrative of its relative newcomer status. Be that as it may, the potential for blockchain to take care of a portion of the real issues we confront today makes it a remarkably energizing and enticing innovation to take after. I will be watching out.

WHAT IS BLOCKCHAIN?

The blockchain is an undeniably artistic development which is realizing an insurgency in the worldwide business advertise. Its advancement has carried with it a more prominent great, for organizations as well as for its recipients also. In any case, since its disclosure to the world, a dream of its operational exercises is as yet misty. The primary inquiry stick in everybody's psyche is - What is Blockchain?

To begin with, Blockchain innovation fills in as a stage that permits the travel of digital data without the danger of being duplicated. It has, as it were, established the framework of a solid spine of another sort of web space. Initially intended to manage Bitcoin - attempting to clarify the layman about the elements of its calculations, the hash capacities, and excellent mark property, today, the innovation buffs are finding other potential employment of this perfect creation which could make ready to the beginning of an entirely new business managing process on the planet.

Blockchain, to characterize in all regards, is a sort of calculation and information dispersion structure for the administration of electronic money without the mediation of any unified organization, modified to record all the budgetary exchanges and also everything that holds esteem.

The Working of Blockchain

Blockchain can be appreciated as Distributed Ledger innovation which was initially formulated to help the Bitcoin digital money. In any case, post overwhelming feedback and dismissal, the innovation was changed for use in things more painful.

To give a reasonable picture, envision a spreadsheet that is expanded tons to times over plenty of figuring frameworks. And afterward, envision that these systems are intended to refresh this spreadsheet occasionally. This is precisely what blockchain is.

Data that is put away on a blockchain is a mutual sheet whose information is accommodated now and again. It's a down to earth way that talks about numerous conspicuous advantages. To being with, the blockchain information doesn't exist in one single place. This implies everything put away in there is open for general visibility and confirmation. Further, there isn't any unified data putting away stage which programmers can degenerate. It's got to over a million processing frameworks one next to the other, and any person can counsel its information with a web association.

Strength and Authenticity of Blockchain

Blockchain innovation is something that minims the web space. It's chic powerful. Like offering information to the overall population through the World Wide Web, squares of real data are put away on blockchain stage which is indistinguishably apparent on all systems.

Crucial to note, blockchain can't be controlled by a solitary people, substance or character, and has nobody purpose of disappointment. Much the same as the web has demonstrated itself as a robust space since most recent 30 years; blockchain too will fill in as a legitimate, dependable worldwide stage for business exchange as it keeps on creating.

Straightforwardness and Incorruptible Nature

Veterans of the business guarantee that blockchain lives in a condition of awareness. It keeps an eye on itself occasionally. It's like a self-evaluating innovation where its system accommodates each exchange, known as a square, which occurs on board at customary interims.

This brings forth two unique properties of blockchain - it's exceptionally straightforward, and in the meantime, it can't be tainted. Every last exchange that happens on this server is implanted inside the system, subsequently, making the whole thing especially unmistakable all the opportunity to general society. Moreover, to alter or exclude data on blockchain requests a humongous measure of endeavors and a substantial processing power. In the midst of this, fakes can be effortlessly distinguished. Henceforth, it's named upright.

Clients of Blockchain

There is indeed not a characterized manage or direction about who will or can make utilization of this flawless innovation. Even though at present, its potential clients are banks, business mammoths, and worldwide economies, the change is open for the everyday exchanges of the overall population also. The main downside blockchain is confronting is global acknowledgment.

BLOCKCHAIN FOR THE IOT IN BUSINESS

A New Horizon in Data Sharing Framework

The blockchain is a mutual disseminated database for distributed exchange. The center of this innovation is bitcoin - a carefully scrambled wallet for controlling transfer and installment framework which was presented in 2009. This exchange administration framework is decentralized and for the most part, keeps running with no go-between. These exchanges are embraced by an arrangement of system hubs and reported in a public record known as blockchain.

The Internet of Things (IoT) is a digital physical system of interconnected registering gadgets, exceptional items, and an individual with one of a kind framework IDs. The target of the IoT space is to serve a sole purpose of reconciliation and exchange information online without the requirement for human or PC obstruction.

There is a mind-boggling connection among blockchain and IoT. IoT giving business elements may discover arrangements utilizing blockchain innovation. The common framework can create and record a cryptographically anchored dataset. Such database and records are ensured against change and robbery, given that it is exceedingly anchored and malware secured. The pair can manufacture straightforwardness and responsibility while directing business advancement components. Blockchain itself can help decrease work environment bungle, overhead cost, and business unconventionality through its interconnected servers. The computerized record can build up a financially savvy business and administration framework where anything can be viably traded appropriately checked and followed. This procedure wipes out the requirement for focal administration framework, which dispenses with numerous bureaucratic red tapes and streamlines business forms. The business reception of this advancement is putting forth immersive stage in IoT space and inside business ventures.

Blockchain enables the interconnected IoT gadgets to share in anchored information trades. Organizations and business substances can utilize blockchain to oversee and process information from edge gadgets, for example, RFID-based resources (Radio-recurrence distinguishing proof), machine discernable scanner tag and QR code, infrared rant (IR Bluster) or device data. Whenever incorporated into business setup, the IoT edge gadgets will have the capacity to exchange the blockchain-based records to refresh contracts or approve correspondence organize. For instance, if an IoT empowered and RFID labeled resource with the touchy geographic area, and secret data moves to another undesignated point, the data will be consequently put away and refreshed on a blockchain record, and necessary moves will be made if the framework is doled out. As the item advances to various areas, the structure enables the partners to get status of the bundle's whereabouts.

To appreciate the product of the blockchain empowered IoT system, business associations need to endure four essential standards:

1. Cost Reduction

The edge gadgets need to diminish task handling time and kill the IoT passages or middle web people inside the framework. Since information sharing and data are conveyed inside the frame, disposing of the new convention, program, equipment, channel, hub or correspondence cuts the overhead expenses.

2. Quickening Data Exchange

Blockchain empowered IoT can wipe out the IoT passage or any separating gadget required to build up organize among cloud, manager, sensors, and devices. Ousting such 'center man' can empower distributed contracts and information sharing. In this procedure, the computerized record wipes out the extra time required for synchronizing gadget and handling and gathering data. Be that as it may, dispensing with the IoT passage gives courses to malicious malware and security break. The blockchain empowered IoT system can handle it by introducing highlights, for example, malware discovery, and encryption motors.

3. Trust Building

Through blockchain empowered IoT space, gadgets and apparatuses can essentially and physically execute and impart as confided in parties. Not at all like an ordinary business where exchanges require underwriting and confirmation, blockchain does not need any focal validation or associate proposal. For whatever length of time that the system is anchored and the confided in parties are mechanically skilled, IoT space does not require additional records. For instance, Team A may not know Team B, might not have met physically or trust irrefutably, but rather the stamped history of online exchanges and data sharing inside block chain's history affirms the business dependability. This empowers the people, associations, and gadgets to procure common trust which is essential to setting up a spinning business setup and wiping out the regulatory mess.

4. Venturing up Security for IoT

Blockchain gives space to decentralized system and innovation that guarantees to store, handle and recover data from its billions of associated gadgets. This framework needs to provide vigorously defended arrange that is both encoded and simple to utilize. The decentralized system needs to provide high throughput, consent, low inertness, and questioning. Introducing blockchain in the IoT system can direct and direct the information trade through the edge gadgets while keeping up the same anchored exchange and data trade of the associated devices.

Disposal of Failure Points in IoT Space

Blockchain empowered IoT can redesign inventory network organize by following the labeled things as they move along different focuses in an import store or distribution center while approving anchored and precise item conveyance. Blockchain establishment gives exact and nitty-gritty item affirmation, and robust traceability of applicable information along the supply chains. As opposed to discovering paper trails for recognizing the nation of the root (COO), IoT can approve every item's physical affirmation using a virtual 'visa' that gives relevant data, for example, credibility and birthplace of the question. Blockchain can likewise make auditable records of the issues and help associations to follow back or deliver the history of the files. It can also give secure access to information organize for official record or elective designs.

Blockchain empowered IoT isn't kept to significant business glitches or utilize cases. Any business element with an IoT space can expand business efficiency by underestimating costs, wiping out bottlenecks, additional cycles, and single purposes of disappointment in the framework by realizing process advancement. It is for such associations as' very own enthusiasm to comprehend, embrace and actualize blockchain to their venture arrangements.

More to Come...

Introduced the fourth modern upset (4IR), blockchain empowered IoT currently establishes the most powerful development after the reconciliation of transistors and registering frameworks. The disturbance respects the 'second machine age' as far as digitization and progressed computerized reasoning (AI). Business confronting associations are the leaders to appreciate the product of this insurgency. It will be shocking if these associations neglect to understand the business facing capability of this uber joining that can convey insight to frameworks anyplace and all over the place. Alongside the new incorporation, this framework additionally escorts fundamental flexibility issues worried about the appropriated system, for example, protection of protection and information organized, coordination of security contraption and administration of licensed innovation. While numerous tech-manufacturers are building an open source establishment to address these issues, associations and business substances should grasp and multiply this innovation for expanded versatility and enhanced item and administration combination.

While the fourth rush of modern insurgency hits the age, among the developing innovations, blockchain is relied upon to without any help upset the business. It has just begun ruling the Internet of Things (IoT) by fusing improved undertaking security, blending business procedures and bringing individuals, gadgets, and associations into a similar biological system. Blockchain empowers the environment to encourage quicker reconciliation of the IoT to arrange and will present scope of prospects for business elements, business associations and people in the following years.

5 WAYS BLOCKCHAIN WILL TRANSFORM THE LIFE OF A COMMON MAN

With the majority of the media set on fire with news of costs of cryptographic forms of money, you may think about how it influences a typical man. Comfortable heart of cryptographic cash and other computerized monetary standards is Blockchain innovation.

There are different modern and regulatory issues that the innovation can unravel for the average man. Do you possess a private company however regularly feel straightforwardness is missing a direct result of common strategies for correspondence? Have you at any point wound up with higher than regular hospital expenses? As an entrepreneur, is finding real competitors a problem for you? These issues influence business people, new companies, private ventures, people and Blockchain innovation tries to give answers to making the life of a typical man substantially more straightforward through streamlined arrangements.

Managing an account

Managing an account in all nations is still extremely centered on paper-serious exchanges for any cash exchange, recordkeeping or other back-end capacities. Blockchain innovation can imitate this in a computerized arrange and make a decentralized record that permits the investors as well as the clients to get to a solitary wellspring of data. This framework enables banks to dispense with odds of extortion as documentation and verification of responsibility for can be checked carefully by financiers in the Blockchain record which can be gotten to whenever in an unalterable organization.

Data fraud is additionally an outstanding issue in the managing an account division, with subjects' data being stolen and used to open deceitful records for illicit exercises. As per the Federal Trade Commission's online database of objections, there have been more than 13 million disputes petitioned for card extortion and wholesale fraud with 3 million of these grumblings being recorded in 2016 alone. Through a blockchain framework, clients can straightforwardly see all records possessed under their name and quickly inform their banks if they detect any suspicious activity in their saving money subtle elements. A portion of the known precedents incorporates IBM-upheld Hyper Ledger Fabric venture and the Utility Settlement Coin by UBS.

Medicinal services

Blockchain innovation can improve therapeutic services in mind-blowing ways and make restorative information administration significantly more straightforward. Making understanding records generally available can permit look into on sedate improvement substantially more advantageous, and it additionally decreases the ramifications of fake medications. Clinical preliminaries and their results can be made accessible in a decentralized system, permitting human services experts and analysts to direct research and discover answers for better therapeutic services. Accenture is one of the most significant organizations that have begun offering inventive social insurance answers for the restorative consideration division for secure and misrepresentation free exchanges.

Medicare cheats can likewise be brought down through blockchain charging administration as the charging framework can be wholly robotized with no extent of mediators submitting false exercises. With more than 56 million individuals under Medicare starting at 2017, over $1.3 billion has been ripped off the legislature through fraudulent practices by recovery offices and home human services administrations. Blockchain frameworks can viably shield residents who look for therapeutic help from medicinal services suppliers that cheat for administrations offered through false charging hones. The real information not just helps medicinal experts in providing treatment in light of the historical backdrop of the patient and his/her family yet it likewise dispenses with the odds of a patient inaccurately remembering past side effects or disarranges.

Open Records

A standout amongst the essential city organization elements of an administration is to record all data about its nationals. This incorporates data about people and organizations concerning their benefits and exercises. The majority of the recorded data is recorded in paper databases, making information administration to a high degree troublesome even in created nations.

Blockchain-based frameworks like Ubiquity can encode every open record in an excellent album to shield the information on residents from being adjusted for false exercises. Data fraud is an issue that can be extremely hard to manage for the organization and digitizing all open data to make it carefully designed can help forestall such cases of criminal movement.

Voting

One of the most significant impediments of the voting framework in relatively every nation is that even today, voters should be physically present at surveying corners to cast their votes and can make things troublesome for individuals who need to movement on survey days. All the more significantly, there are no methods for confirming the survey results for the average native.

Blockchain advancement organizations like Followmyvote are thinking of arrangements that look to make internet voting a reality. It will enable residents to see precise data on survey standings and results and different measurements openly. It likewise prompts more secure voting in favor of residents of nations in the inner or outer clash, and criminal exercises to constrain nationals into voting in favor of particular competitors can be evaded.

Business Hiring

Organizations of all sizes experience serious difficulties finding the correct staff. Through blockchain innovation, it is workable for organizations to check qualifications of all candidates through an advanced database. Blockchain innovation can be connected to make a decentralized database of experts with tested capabilities in a safe record that organizations can allude to for enlisting hopefuls. Learning Machine is a New-York based organization that tries to address this issue centers around recording evident data on specialists.

Duty or work-related cheats make up 34% of all data fraud starting at 2016, and a blockchain framework makes the procuring procedure for any business substantially more secure as an organization would approach legitimate hopefuls just, lessening the danger of contracting deceitful representatives. It likewise enables candidates by accelerating the procuring to process and helping them to discover occupations they are qualified for and have a problem-free application process.

Utilization of blockchain advancements helps people and organizations alike, and it likewise ensures individual data while making critical information freely noticeable. While blockchain has the best application in digital money, its utilization can spread to different parts also to give significant answers to natives around the globe.

IS BLOCKCHAIN TECHNOLOGY THE FUTURE OF THE INTERNET?

1. Executing Trusted Third Parties:

Blockchain the perpetual, mixed, decentralized - the record has a capacity of making each real strategy, activity, and affiliation self-decision. This infers we can discard go-betweens, specialists, and beat the trust of outsiders. In this way, streamlining every business, organization and non-advantage development.

The back and forth movement scene of home advances require a staggering snare of title looks, title assurance, and grand minor trade charges that are critical to keeping the system running. These structures exist because, genuinely, the trading of land has been a system that requires a great deal of trust in dated records. In any case, the Blockchain would address these stresses, and a specific property's record can contain an illustrious and endorsed history of trades, constraining the necessity for establishments to give chance help and place stock in organizations, rather the trade can exist in its own right.

2. Blockchain in 2018 - past Bitcoin:

The sensitive change of Bitcoin in 2017 moved the persevering quality, and excellent conditions of the necessary improvement utilized by this propelled money, the blockchain. In 2017, blockchain changed into the second most standard look word, and scattered record progression will keep getting significance transversely completed different industries. Blockchain tries will beat passed on figuring and IoT in financing hypothesis. Nations with official blockchain procedures, similar to Malta, are relied upon to wind up driving close by business sectors.

3. Ensuring a Secure Internet of the Future:

One of the essential favorable circumstances that blockchain gives over other record writing computer programs is that it relies upon cryptography and is adjusted to be constant, one can't retreat to a particular point on the blockchain and change information. For the ten years of block chain's quality, it has never been hacked and will proceed so until the end when the innovation lives.

4. Blockchain for Digital Advertising:

Electronic publicizing faces challenges, for instance, space blackmail, bot development, nonattendance of straightforwardness and broad portion models. The issue is that impulses are not balanced, making the two promoters and distributors feel they are on the losing side of the game plan. The blockchain is the response for the pass on straightforwardness to the store organize since it passes typically on trust to a trustless circumstance.

5. The Effect of Streaming Money on Business:

We have ended up being so familiar with the fortnightly or frequently booked finance interim that we accept this as a given in business and as laborers. Anyway 2018 engravings the year when this isn't any more a required standard. One especially empowering nature of blockchain advancement is scaled down scale portions. Another is sharp contracts. These can participate in entrancing highways, one of which is to make spilling money. Notwithstanding the way, this was foreseen a long time back the truth is occurring not surprisingly now

At last, blockchain is a great innovation to use to store vast proportions of necessary documentation in adventures, for instance, human administrations, collaborations, copyright and some more. Blockchain removes the necessity for an operator concerning approving contracts.

HOW CAN BLOCKCHAIN INCREASE YOUR PROFIT IN BANKING?

Each industry is altering by innovation in the digital economy and has brought about extreme changes. The managing an accounting industry is the same. Banks have adequately grasped the eventual fate of digitization. We are on the pinnacle of a desperate insurgency, but most are uninformed. Indeed, even those people that welcome the capability of blockchain innovation regularly look no more remote than bitcoins. Once an individual burrow further and sees how blockchain capacities and its suggestions they will unavoidably understand its significance.

The blockchain is a disseminated record that holds a far-reaching and an unedited recording of all significant data identified with an advanced exchange. This record permits to settle transactions in a flash and immovable. The blockchain is a blockbuster in managing an account as it lessens the period it takes to finish an installment and disposes of repetitive procedures. Blockchain innovation can agitate keeping the money. In our current reality where billions of individuals don't approach banks, blockchain innovation can have a profound effect. Inhabitants of creating nations with restricted access to saving money would get an opportunity to make a record and make exchanges at a universal level. It will likewise empower residents to have a protected and confided in exchanges between members without the requirement for a concentrated checking or a middle person.

It is nothing unexpected that money-related establishments are investigating the one of a kind capacity of the blockchain. The monetary associations can likewise utilize it to increase enhanced knowledge into advertising moves and increment straightforwardness. Blockchain innovation can diminish the bank's foundation costs and empower quicker handling time. Information administration is a significant issue in managing an account, yet with the assistance of blockchain innovation, banks can store any information, and enable that information to be gotten to just as per the predefined rules.

Exchange fund is a unique region inside saving money that could change because of blockchain innovation. The obsolete procedures in the managing account territories should be refreshed, as far as cost and proficiency. The blockchain is the best stage to unite parties in an anchored arrange without an outsider and by making every exchange safely.

Regardless of whether it's installments, snappy exchanges or straightforwardness, block chain's basic properties of proficiency, cost-adequacy and secure exchanges are a couple of motivations to the developing fame of this innovation over the money related associations. Blockchain innovation is potential enough to change the whole arrangement of the Banking. Be that as it may, significantly more should be improved the situation money related associations and inhabitants to end up utterly mindful of the suggestions and advantages of the blockchain. In any case, there is almost certainly that blockchain innovation holds the way to enhance the keeping money framework. Using this innovation can acquire numerous powerful advantages the managing an accounting industry.

The blockchain is fundamentally changing the ventures, upgrading client encounter, and reforming the trust crosswise over organizations. Bitcoin and other virtual monetary standards fame are as of now demonstrating block chain's value in a fund and managing an account ventures. However, this disseminated record innovation does not stop itself here. How about we distill the main five businesses Blockchain will make a raid in.

Keeping money, Finance, and Insurance

The blockchain is infusing improved security and data partaking in the managing an accounting industry which in every case needs a top of a digitized and anchored condition with the goal that it can fill in as basic storage facilities and exchange centers of significant worth. The blockchain is advocating its promising job in the money related administrations economy in changing ways. Numerous banks have likewise set out upon this innovation including Swiss bank UBS and UK-based Barclays.

Retail and Consumer Goods

Blockchain items in retail and web-based business enterprises are going about as a hesitant for impediments and as an impetus for expanding permeability of customer items. By utilizing a dispersed and confided in the database, blockchain arrangements are decreasing the hindrances that obstruct efficient tedious settlement forms and guaranteeing more prominent straightforwardness through a mutual, changeless record that empowers organizations to build up a solid trust crosswise over zones like invoicing and installments, inventory network, and worldwide delivery.

Social insurance

This disturbing innovation is expanding the security, protection and, interoperability of wellbeing information by keeping the persistent, focused biological system in the center. This innovation is heading off to the edges to give another model to wellbeing data trades (HIE) by making EMRs electronic medicinal records more effective, disintermediated, and anchored.

Taxpayer-supported organizations

The robust, complex functionalities of blockchain have caught the eyeballs of government everywhere throughout the world. The potential utilizes situations, where the legislature is foreseeing the utilization of this hyper ledger innovation, are social insurance, assess and Internal Revenue Monitoring, National Identity Management Systems, Secure Banking Services, and electronic voting framework.

Production network Management

In SCM industry, exchanges can be archived into a changeless decentralized record and can be checked in a more anchored manner while keeping up end-to-end straightforwardness, thus helping in diminishing time postponements and human mistakes. It can likewise be utilized in testing the legitimacy and exchange status of items by following them from their dispatch focuses.

Other than this, hyper ledger innovation is being devoured by systems administration industry, shared ridesharing applications, distributed storage, media outlet, informing use, land, basic framework security, swarm subsidizing and some more. In any case, the five parts we have talked about above best the diagram, however.

Trusting that, the decentralized digital money can take care of the world's most exceedingly bad issues; each industry should welcome blockchain innovation into their organizations and begin making changes and future headways. Contract a stable blockchain application improvement organization and start building more prominent incentive for your association.

25 REAL EXAMPLES OF HOW BLOCKCHAIN IS CHANGING OUR WORLD

Cybersecurity

1. Guardtime – This company is creating "keyless" signature systems using blockchain which is currently used to secure the health records of one million Estonian citizens.

REMME is a decentralized authentication system which aims to replace logins and passwords with SSL certificates stored on a blockchain.

Healthcare

2. Gem – This startup is working with the Centre for Disease Control to put disease outbreak data onto a blockchain which it says will increase the effectiveness of disaster relief and response.

3. SimplyVital Health – Has two health-related blockchain products in development, ConnectingCare which tracks the progress of patients after they leave the hospital, and Health Nexus, which aims to provide decentralized blockchain patient records.

4. MedRec – An MIT project involving blockchain electronic medical records designed to manage authentication, confidentiality and data sharing.

Financial services

5. ABRA – A cryptocurrency wallet which uses the Bitcoin blockchain to hold and track balances stored in different currencies.

6. Bank Hapoalim – A collaboration between the Israeli bank and Microsoft to create a blockchain system for managing bank guarantees.

7. Maersk – The shipping and transport consortium has unveiled plans for a blockchain solution for streamlining marine insurance.

8. Aeternity – Allows the creation of smart contracts which become active when network consensus agrees that conditions have been met – allowing for automated payments to be made when parties agree that conditions have been met, for example.

Manufacturing and industrial

9. Provenance – This project aims to provide a blockchain-based provenance record of transparency within supply chains.

10. Jiocoin – India's biggest conglomerate, Reliance Industries, has said that it is developing a blockchain-based supply chain logistics platform along with its own cryptocurrency, Jiocoin.

11. Hijro – Previously known as Fluent, aims to create a blockchain framework for collaborating on prototyping and proof-of-concept.

12. SKUChain – Another blockchain system for allowing tracking and tracing of goods as they pass through a supply chain.

13. STORJ.io – Distributed and encrypted cloud storage, which allows users to share unused hard drive space.

Government

14. Dubai – Dubai has set sights on becoming the world's first blockchain-powered state. In 2016 representatives of 30 government departments formed a committee dedicated to investigating opportunities across health records, shipping, business registration and preventing the spread of conflict diamonds.

15. South Korea – Samsung is creating blockchain solutions for the South Korean government which will be put to use in public safety and transport applications.

16. Govcoin – The UK Department of Work and Pensions is investigating using blockchain technology to record and administer benefit payments.

Charity

17. Bitgive – This service aims to provide greater transparency to charity donations and clearer links between giving and project outcomes. It is working with established charities including Save The Children, The Water Project and Medic Mobile.

Retail

18. OpenBazaar – OpenBazaar is an attempt to build a decentralized market where goods and services can be traded with no middle-man.

19. Loyyal – This is a blockchain-based universal loyalty framework, which aims to allow consumers to combine and trade loyalty rewards in new ways, and retailers to offer more sophisticated loyalty packages.

20. Blockpoint.io – Allows retailers to build payment systems around blockchain currencies such as

Bitcoin, as well as blockchain derived gift cards and loyalty schemes.

Real Estate

21. Ubiquity – This startup is creating a blockchain-driven system for tracking the complicated legal process which creates friction and expense in real estate transfer.

Transport and Tourism

22. IBM Blockchain Solutions – IBM has said it will go public with a number of non-finance related blockchain initiatives with global partners in 2018. This video envisages how efficiencies could be driven in the vehicle leasing industry.

23. Webjet – The online travel portal is developing a blockchain solution to allow stock of empty hotel rooms to be efficiently tracked and traded, with

payment fairly routed to the network of middle-men sites involved in filling last-minute vacancies.

Media

24. Kodak – Kodak recently sent its stock soaring after announcing that it is developing a blockchain system for tracking intellectual property rights and payments to photographers.

25. Ujomusic – Founded by singer-songwriter Imogen Heap to record and track royalties for musicians, as well as allowing them to create a record of ownership of their work.

CHAPTER TWO

AN INTRODUCTION TO THE BLOCKCHAIN TECHNOLOGY FOR THE BEGINNERS

Nowadays, innovation is scaling more up to date statures of achievement at an unimaginably quick pace. One of the most recent triumphs toward this path is the advancement of the Blockchain innovation. The innovation has incredibly affected the back segment. Indeed, it was at first produced for Bitcoin - the electronic money. Be that as it may, now, it discovers its application in various things also.

Running over this far was presumably simple. Be that as it may, one is yet to know what Blockchain is.

A disseminated database

Envision an electronic spreadsheet, which is replicated umpteen number of times over a PC arrange. Presently, envision the PC arrange outlined so keenly that it frequently refreshes the worksheet all alone. This is an expansive diagram of the Blockchain. Blockchain holds data as a common database. Also, this database gets continuously accommodated.

This methodology has its very own advantages. It doesn't enable the database to be put away at any single area. The records in it have honest to open goodness quality and can be confirmed conclusively. As there's no unified adaptation of the documents, unapproved clients have no way to control with and degenerate the information. The Blockchain disseminated database is at the same time facilitated by a great many PCs, making the info effectively open to nearly anybody over the virtual web.

To make the idea or the innovation clearer, it is a smart thought to talk about the Google Docs similarity.

Google Docs similarity for Blockchain

After the appearance of the email, the regular method for sharing archives is to send a Microsoft Word doc as the connection to a beneficiary or beneficiaries. The recipients will set aside their sweet opportunity to experience it before they send back the reconsidered duplicate. In this methodology, one needs to hold up until getting the arrival duplicate to see the progressions made to the archive. This happens because the sender is bolted out from making rectifications till the beneficiary is finished with the altering and sends the report back. Contemporary databases don't permit two proprietors to get to a similar record in the meantime. This is the means by which banks keep up equalizations of their customers or record holders.

As opposed to the set practice, Google docs permit both the gatherings to get to a similar archive in the meantime. Besides, it additionally allows seeing an only form of the record to them two all the while. Much the same as a mutual record, the Google Docs moreover goes about as a collective archive. The dispersed part ends up significant when the sharing includes various clients. The Blockchain innovation is, as it were, an expansion of this idea. In any case, it is essential to call attention to here that the Blockchain isn't intended to share records. Or maybe, it is only a similarity, which will have obvious thought regarding this front-line innovation.

Notable Blockchain highlights

Blockchain stores squares of data over the system that are indistinguishable. By ethicalness of this element:

Any single, specific substance can't control the information or data.

There can't be any single disappointment point either.

The information is held in an open system, which guarantees total straightforwardness in the general strategy.

The information put away in it can't be undermined.

Interest for Blockchain designers

As expressed before, Blockchain innovation has a high application in the realm of a fund and keeping the money. As per the World Bank, more than US$ 430 billion cash exchanges were sent through it just in 2015. In this way, Blockchain designers have a critical interest in the market.

The Blockchain disposes of the result of the brokers in such money-related exchanges. It was the innovation of the GUI (Graphical User Interface), which encouraged the average man to get to PCs in the type of work areas. Likewise, the wallet application is the most widely recognized GUI for the Blockchain innovation. Clients make utilization of the wallet to purchase things they need utilizing Bitcoin or some other cryptographic money.

BLOCKCHAIN: THE NEXT LEVEL OF SECURITY TO CRM

'Blockchain' is the new drifting most recent innovation that is developing these days. It is an idea that guarantees the security of information utilizing 'cryptography.' It is a persistent developing rundown of records called squares, which are connected to one another inside by commonly containing a cryptographic hash code of the past square.

"Blockchain essentially is an open, circulated advanced record that can record exchanges between two gatherings effectively security. It takes after shared architecture (decentralized and conveyed)".

How Blockchain guarantees the most significant amount of security? Or then again how it functions?

Blockchain can give the most elevated level of security that is the reason it has been utilized to store value-based information. It works in a way like not long after the original square has been made, each adjoining hinder in the record uses the past square's hash to compute its very own hash. Before any expansion of another square to the chain, the genuineness and uniqueness must be checked by a computational procedure. What's more, this procedure additionally incorporates the authorization and affirmation of alternate obstructs that the recently included square has been confirmed. This procedure of approval moreover guarantees that all duplicates of the conveyed record share a similar state.

Because of this system of including hash code and checks, the recently covered square can be referenced in resulting squares; however, it can't be changed. If somebody endeavors to swap out or hamper a square, the hashes for past and resulting squares will likewise get change and disturb the record's shared state. At whatever point this circumstance happen different PCs in the system know that an issue has occurred and no new squares will be added to the chain until the end that the problem is unraveled. And afterward, the square causing the mistake will be disposed of, and the entire procedure of approval will get rehashed.

In what capacity can Blockchain advantage CRM?

With CRM programming Blockchain can include energizing information security features (options). The mix of CRM with Blockchain empowers association to have verified (or visible) records which are anchored by Blockchain innovation. Mainly if the CRM is cloud-based.

That implies it can profit CRM application by confining the entrance to track information from undesirable sources. Right now, CRM clients over the globe confront the issues of copy or erroneous information. Since, Blockchain innovation stores information in the types of squares so it could enable a client to possess a different square that speaks to interestingly to them and their data, related exchange subtle elements, and other relevant information.

Blockchain limits the copy or hazardous information from hampering the database, and consequently, it accelerates CRM forms and guarantees clients fulfillment.

The blockchain alludes to an open record innovation in which every cryptographic money exchange is carefully marked to affirm its creativity and guarantee that the data in that isn't messed with. The tasks recorded on the blockchain and the record itself are thought to be of the most abnormal amount of trustworthiness.

At the beginning of cryptographic money, individuals felt that blockchain was about bitcoin. Today, it is quickly getting to be clear that the innovation is about something beyond bitcoin, or computerized monetary forms so far as that is concerned. Be that as it may, while blockchain can change almost every industry, no place will its effect be more articulated than in philanthropic giving.

For philanthropy associations, blockchain presents an original window for straightforwardness and trustworthiness, which could help make them more reliable according to benefactors. A portion of the issues that charities think about include absence of responsibility for how cash is spent and straightforwardness. Givers are now and then hesitant to give since they can't make sure where their assets are going to or their identity assisting with their gift. After some time, such concerns can make them wind up disillusioned.

This makes it hard for philanthropy associations to draw in supports or hold them. Blockchain is quick bringing trust up in the framework by indicating givers where their cash is going. The innovation accomplishes this by making the structure entirely straightforward and data, effortlessly open. Here are the means by which blockchain upgrades straightforwardness and trust in foundations:

Assets go straightforwardly to the reason contributors are contributing towards. On account of blockchain innovation, gifts require not go through go-betweens anymore. Instead, they go straight to the beneficiaries and the organizations that are in a situation to help them. This assistance guarantees that there's less space for misrepresentation or money related spillage in the framework and that monies aren't going into the wrong pockets. The outcome is that benefactors feel more urged to give.

All exchanges are traceable. Circulated records can be utilized to track transactions. Such enhanced traceability makes it simpler to screen how reserves are being spent. Thus, contributors can see even from a separation, how their assets wound up helping the general population that philanthropy establishments guarantee to help.

Blockchain makes it less demanding to differentiate good-natured associations one from the other from fake ones. Since gifts influenced utilizing digital forms of money to can be followed, it ends up simpler for benefactors to recognize the associations that are advancing their motivation from those that look to advance a couple of people. Along these lines, they become acquainted with the correct philanthropies to work with.

In general, blockchain and digital money will help guarantee proficiency and give sponsor certainty that their gift is being put toward the reason that they bolster.

Benevolent associations need to grasp the innovation on the off chance that they intend to enhance straightforwardness and additionally track and exchange reserves rapidly. It is for every one of these reasons that stages, for example, Sony try to assist Businesses with delivering more prominent straightforwardness and trust through the blockchain innovation.

The Future of Blockchain Technology

What is Blockchain?

The term blockchain has been utilized in various social and corporate discussions as of late, and everybody appears to have found out about blockchain innovation, yet a dominant part of the populace has no clue what it implies.

With the goal for us to clarify what blockchain innovation implies enable us to give you a short breakdown of the historical backdrop of how the exchange of cash has advanced. Honestly at whatever point individuals used to trade significant things, there were center men whose sole reason for existing was to record the credibility of the two gatherings and fabricate trust between them. Presently these center men are known as banks. The utilization of banks and merchants has proceeded after some time and with the development of electronic resources like stock, electronic cash, and licensed innovation the requirement for a more secure strategy has risen. This is on account of electronic resources usually record inside a PC that is along these lines helpless against control and burglary. In this manner the utilization of the blockchain innovation empowers gatherings to execute straightforwardly and straightforwardly guaranteeing that the trade is secure and proficient.

The Future of Bitcoin

Blockchain has the capacity of totally disturbing the financial business the same was online networking upset predominant press or a similar way Netflix demolished Blockbuster films. Blockchain innovation has the capability of being utilized as a stage that gives budgetary administrations to everybody concerning the world; this incorporates individuals in creating nations who might not have the entrance to conventional keeping money benefits and can't manage the cost of the rates required to make extensive exchanges. This innovation has the capability of making real leaps forward in about every real industry that are generally controlled by large enterprises.

The utilization of Blockchain innovation in Education

Blockchain innovation in instruction can be utilized to make sense of the understudies that require the grants and the individuals who can manage the cost of it. This is on account of a couple of understudies have been bypassing the framework and getting financing. This would wind up being contrary to the penniless understudies who wind up dropping out or gathering a great deal of obligation that makes them work for about.

Ultimately, the countless populace may as of now be concealing their heads in the sand as they wish blockchain to leave this bit of innovation, however, is undoubtedly going no place. Sooner rather than later we will all exchange utilizing blockchain as a significant aspect of our everyday exercises our extraordinary grandkids will read about cash and ATMs similarly as how we learned about the deal exchange and gold. It is along these lines primary that we hop on the temporary fad at the earliest opportunity and get balanced before we are compelled to change.

IS BLOCKCHAIN THE LATEST REVOLUTION IN TECHNOLOGY?

The blockchain is more similar to a computerized record to store money related exchanges simply like a book that contains what comes in and what goes out. Not at all like current document, is the computerized one significantly more tremendous and secure without any middle people included.

In Blockchain, each square contains, however not constrained to, a cryptographic hash of the past square alongside the exchange information. It very well may be utilized by two gatherings to record exchanges in a safe and lasting way. It is overseen by a shared system and permits the safe travel of digital data.

For what reason is Blockchain the most recent unrest in innovation?

Blockchain innovation was initially intended to manage Bitcoin yet now it has turned into all the rage, an upheaval. Amid its previous stage, the change faced overwhelming feedback and dismissal however after an astute update, and it turned out to be more painful, more valuable, and more secure. It has now turned into a useful method to store information in a digital frame that is accommodated every once in a while.

How about we investigate a portion of the advantages:

Credibility - The data is put away in hinders that are additionally put away on Blockchain that can't be controlled by a solitary individual or personality. It just implies that there are no or exceptionally fewer odds of disappointment and the innovation can fill in as a dependable space for business exchange.

Straightforwardness - The technically knowledgeable individuals guarantee that the Blockchain innovation is entirely straightforward. As the squares are recorded and added to it in the subsequent request, the members can monitor the exchanges effortlessly and without recordkeeping.

Quality - if there should be an occurrence of an anomaly, a Blockchain framework makes it less demanding for concerned celebrated to explore any issue as the structure can lead them the distance to its purpose of the starting point. The quality affirmation makes it a perfect innovation for parts where following the start and other critical aspects of interest are essential.

No Tampering - As the exchanges and records are confirmed every time they are passed on starting with one square then onto the next, there are less or no odds of blunder. The precision of the procedure shields the information from altering, making the innovation more comfortable to use and effective.

Coordinated - In the period when the time is cash, Blockchain can assume a primary job by permitting quicker dealings. As the framework does not require a protracted procedure of confirmation and leeway, it very well may be utilized by various ventures for settling the negotiations quick.

Cost Saving - Last not the minimum, Blockchain is a financially savvy innovation since it doesn't include an outsider. It made the framework a perfect one for the two new companies and built up associations.

Well! The time has come to comprehend the innovation and its advantages previously applying it to any business...

4 WAYS BLOCKCHAIN WILL DISRUPT BUSINESS AS WE KNOW IT

Blockchain innovation and digital currencies like Bitcoin created a ton of news this previous year. It appears as though consistently there's another feature touting an up and coming insurgency or making light of this innovation as a trend with few long-haul prospects. If you are new to blockchain tech or are as yet fabricating a perspective, let me put forth the defense for unrest.

Formula for Disruption

How about we begin with why we trust working with an organization. We believe our biggest retailers to satisfy our buys to convey products and enterprises. We think our banks will guarantee our record balance is right and exchanges are checked and free of misrepresentation. The frameworks these organizations have set up assemble our trust. For instance, directions, hostile to misrepresentation frameworks and administrations that confirm exchanges all assume a job in guaranteeing business is led above board. Visa organizations are a particular case of an outsider that charges an expense on each buy to confirm and settle customer credit. Generally speaking, every one of these gatherings goes about as brokers and give their administrations to a charge on every exchange.

The quantity of exchanges in our worldwide economy is marvelous. Overall retail deals are more than $20 trillion every year, and gross world item (GWP) is over $100 trillion. So tremendous quantities of arrangements and exchanges utilize brokers and their confirmation administrations to run confided in organizations. As the expense of working together, we acknowledge that these mediators extricate charges on a considerable number of exchanges to control misrepresentation and keep up customer confidence. Those costs creep into the economy, driving up everyday costs and the costs for merchandise and enterprises.

In any case, what might occur if there were less expensive or quicker approaches to check bargains in our economy? If substitutes exist, the funds would be in the trillions of dollars. For instance, online installment passages win a large number by including over 2.9% every exchange. There's likewise the expense of lost time. Mediators all include days and long stretches of postponements in the land, credit endorsements or permit restorations. Cutting the costs put in on each arrangement and request in the economy would return unbelievable benefits to organizations and upset the manner in which we participate in trade. Infusing reserve funds in the trillions would kick begin development in the worldwide economy bigger than what anyone government or organization could do individually?

In comes the blockchain

Blockchain innovation is necessarily a decentralized framework for recording dependable exchanges with no go-betweens. Utilizing the intensity of cryptography, every transaction is undeniably connected to one another and shared all through a system of PCs. PCs on the network naturally confirm the terms of exchanges, going about as moment bookkeepers "checking the books" with no charges. So programmed check of transactions is the essential element of blockchain innovation.

This is the manner by which digital forms of money like Bitcoin work as well. There are a limited number of coins earned through understanding computational riddles or buying them from another person. Somebody with the answer for a question can demonstrate their responsibility for the currency because their verification is recorded in the first blockchain organize. Members of the system cryptographically confirm the character, and the trustworthiness of one another's evidence to ensure who possesses which coins.

The effect of the blockchain idea is apparent. Utilizing blockchain innovation, organizations could spare trillions and convey benefits quicker. In particular, they could:

Dispense with the expenses of demonstrating exchanges are real from outsider administrations, saving trillions every year.

Empower quicker administration by in a flash checking the terms of exchanges, evacuating agent's administrations like banks, governments, and commercial centers.

Convey all the more safely, utilizing the security incorporated with the blockchain without advance speculation.

Computerize more convoluted organizations, similar to protection administrations, utilizing modified "Shrewd Contracts."

HOW BLOCKCHAIN WORKS

The blockchain is a bit of programming intended to make decentralized databases.

The framework is altogether "open source," implying that anybody can see, alter and propose changes to its underlying code base.

While it has turned out to be progressively well known on account of Bitcoin's development - it's been around since 2008, making it around ten years (old in figuring terms).

The essential point about "blockchain" is that it was intended to make applications that don't require focal information preparing administration. This implies in case you're utilizing a framework expand over it (to be specific Bitcoin) - your information will be put away on 1,000's of "autonomous" servers around the globe (not possessed by any focal administration).

The manner in which the administration works is by making a "record." This record enables clients to make "exchanges" with one another - having the substance of those exchanges put away in new "squares" of each "blockchain" database.

Contingent upon the application making the exchanges, they ought to be scrambled with various calculations. Since this encryption utilizes cryptography to "scramble" the information put away in each new "square," the expression "crypto" portrays the procedure of cryptographically anchoring any new blockchain information that an application may make.

To ultimately see how it functions, you should value that "blockchain" isn't innovation - it just uses innovation in a somewhat unique manner. Its center is an information diagram known as "Merkle trees." Merkle trees are routed for PC frameworks to store sequentially requested "adaptations" of an informational index, enabling them to oversee persistent moves up to that information.

The reason this is imperative is on account of current "information" frameworks are what could be portrayed as "2D" - meaning they don't have any approach to track updates profoundly dataset. The information is permanently kept altogether as it is - with any updates explicitly connected to it. While there's nothing amiss with this, it poses an issue in that it implies that information either must be refreshed physically or his extremely hard to upgrade.

The arrangement that "blockchain" gives is the formation of "variants" of the information. Each "square" added to a "chain" (a "chain" being a database) gives a rundown of new exchanges for that information. This implies in case you're ready to integrate this usefulness with a framework which encourages the exchange of information between at least two clients (informing and so forth), you'll have the capacity to make an altogether free structure.

This is the thing that we've seen with any semblance of Bitcoin. In opposition to prevalent thinking, Bitcoin isn't a "cash" in itself; it's an open record of money related exchanges.

This open record is scrambled with the goal that just the members in the exchanges can see/alter the information (henceforth the name "crypto")... in any case, progressively along these lines, the way that the information is put away on, and handled by 1,000's of servers around the globe implies the administration can work free of any banks (its fundamental draw).

Issues with Bitcoin's hidden thought and so on aside, the support of the administration is that it's mostly a framework that works over a system of handling machines (called "diggers"). These are on the whole running the "blockchain" programming - and work to "incorporate" new exchanges into "hinders" that keeps the Bitcoin database as a la mode as could reasonably be expected.

While numerous individuals have indiscriminately promised help for blockchain, it's got various vulnerabilities - most outstandingly that it depends as a rule on the encryption calculations utilized by its different applications. If one of these calculations fizzles, or clients are endangered in any capacity, the whole "blockchain" framework could endure subsequently.

Blockchain Web Hosting

The striking ongoing increment in Bitcoin costs has revived the creative energy of numerous financial specialists, yet Blockchain innovation isn't only about the cash. In this section, we will investigate how noteworthy an effect this continuous innovation will have on exemplary web facilitating administrations.

The idea of cryptographic money isn't advanced science. This medium of trade is not any drunker than the current salary. In any case, it, in any case, needs a safe and confiding in a condition in which it can work, and Blockchain gives that.

What is Blockchain? Numerous false impressions are identifying with it, at the same time, for the motivations behind this part, we will characterize it as an appropriated spreadsheet. We are altogether comfortable with Excel or

Open Office spreadsheets, yet what makes Blockchain so appealing is how it is allocated.

Much the same as the records in Torrent, Blockchain is a shared system where it isn't essential to guarantee trust between parties. On account of present-day cryptography, the faith is instead kept up on the level of a single record as opposed to the gathering facilitating it.

Approve, so now we comprehend the nuts and bolts of the digital currency upset, yet how, we may ask, does it influence web facilitating administrations? Basically, in its least heavy frame, this would propose not just offering your administrations in your nearby cash, yet also in Bitcoin and different digital currencies.

In any case, this isn't the finish of the unrest. Bitcoin and other advanced monetary standards require electronic wallets to work, and there is in this way the massive potential for conventional web facilitating merchants. If you have the trust of your clients and are promoting their locales, at that point why not have their electronic valets?

Every task in digital currency is an accepted exchange between two electronic valets. Each trade is kept up through the wallet, and you can likewise give an interface to your clients to get to it. This factor is crucial with a specific end goal to completely comprehend the effect Blockchain can have on your web facilitating business.

The blockchain isn't just about cash. The most up to date forms of its conventions additionally give the chance to authorize an agreement between the gatherings, regardless of whether this is a membership to satellite TV or surely some other sort of bill. They all should be put away someplace, and there is a place for web facilitating organizations to be included.

BRINGING SCIENTIFIC RIGOR TO MEDICAL RESEARCH USING BLOCKCHAIN TECHNOLOGY

Blockchain innovation connected to medicinal research can enhance trust in science by making an unchangeable, time-stamped record of the exploration discoveries. Blockchain innovation, concocted by Satoshi Nakamoto in 2008, guarantees that exchanges went into a file can't be changed with time. As connected to the cryptographic money bitcoin (BTC), the outcome is a financial framework that, can't be controlled by an incorporated government since it makes a permanent and precise record all things considered. The quality of the structure originates from its utilization of a dispersed database when contrasted with current fiscal structures that require a concentrated database, for example, is utilized with Visa organizations and banks. Applying this same innovation to restorative research builds trust in the outcomes because merely like bitcoin, the exchanges (logical information gathered) are for all time documented in an unchangeable, changeless way.

The trading of cash, much the same as the lead of medicinal research, requires an abnormal state of trust. Money in the past has produced this trust through government directions and national bank oversight. Therapeutic research in the history has endeavored to make high amounts of confidence through associate audit directed by respectable restorative diaries, for example, the New England Journal of Medicine. The two strategies for producing belief depend on a confided in focal expert, either the legislature or a restorative diary. In that capacity, the two approaches are exceptionally helpless to misrepresentation using defilement or innocent mistakes of the brought together expert. This has prompted far-reaching doubt in therapeutic research. Bitcoin works unexpectedly since it sets up a technique for depending on a dispersed system in light of a scientific calculation, instead of concentrated specialist vulnerable to human blunder.

Budgetary exchanges require may be the most significant amount of trust. Individuals need to realize that all transactions recorded in the record be altogether exact and impervious to being changed later on. Since blockchain innovation as actualized in bitcoin has earned this trust, bitcoin has turned into a generally utilized store of significant worth with a market capitalization of over USD 100 billion. At the point when different digital forms of money are viewed as the aggregate trust in blockchain based budgetary frameworks surpass USD 250 billion. Also, human services experts should have the capacity to assume that information got from restorative research is both precise and permanent. Doctors need to realize that therapeutic research isn't copied or deceitful in any position. Blockchain innovation has made bitcoin a trusted, worldwide cash. Similarly, blockchain based restorative research will extraordinarily expand trust in the outcomes and therefore, enhanced therapeutic consideration.

How Blockchain Can Re-Invent the Global Supply Chain

After it rose in 2008, the innovation behind the world's most famous cryptographic money, Bitcoin, held court on the edges, drawing in consideration for the most part from new companies and the budgetary administrations segment. In any case, it has as of late gotten a considerable measure of compensation as organizations bit by bit to acknowledge it could be important for some different things other than following installments.

A blockchain is a conveyed record that sorts exchanges into squares. Each square is fastened to the one preceding it, utilizing modern math, the distance back to the first transaction. Passages are lasting, straightforward, and accessible, which makes it feasible for network individuals to see exchange narratives completely. Each refresh establishes another "square," added to the finish of the "chain" - a structure that makes it troublesome for anybody to alter the records at a later stage. The document enables data to be recorded and shared between large gatherings of foreign organizations, and all individuals should, by and large, approve any updates - which is to everybody's most significant advantage.

To date, much consideration and cash have been spent on commercial applications for the innovation. Be that as it may, a similarly encouraging experiment lies with global inventory network connections, whose intricacy and the decent variety of interests present precisely the sorts of difficulties this innovation looks to address.

A necessary use of the blockchain worldview to the inventory network could be to enlist the exchange of merchandise on the record, as transfers would recognize the gatherings required, and additionally the value, date, area, quality and condition of the item and whatever other data that would be applicable to dealing with the store network. The cryptography-based and changeless nature of the exchanges would make it about challenging to trade off the record.

Presently, a considerable number of new businesses and organizations are sending blockchain to re-create their worldwide inventory network and maintain their organizations all the more effectively:

1. For Maersk, the world's most significant transportation organization, the test isn't following the commonplace rectangular delivery holders that sail the world on board payload ships. Instead, it is circumnavigating the mountains of printed material related with every compartment. A separate compartment can require stamps and endorsements from upwards of 30 parties, including traditions, charge authorities and wellbeing experts, spread crosswise over at least 200 associations. While holders can be stacked on a ship in a matter of minutes, a compartment can be held up at the port for a considerable length of time because a bit of paper disappears, while the merchandise inside the ruin. The expense of moving and monitoring this printed material frequently squares with the loss of physically running the holder around the globe. The framework is likewise overflowing with extortion as the import bill of replenishing can be altered, or replicated, giving lawbreakers a chance to redirect merchandise or flow fake items, prompting billions of dollars in sea misrepresentation every year.

The previous summer, Maersk has looked for participation from traditions experts, cargo forwarders and the makers that fill the holders. It started running its first preliminaries of another computerized transporting record with these accomplices, for transportation courses among Rotterdam and Newark. In the wake of approving an archive, the traditions experts could instantly transfer a duplicate of it, with a digital signature, so every other person included - including Maersk itself and other government specialists - could see that it was finished. If there was debate later, everybody could return to the record and be sure that nobody had modified it meanwhile. The cryptography included likewise makes it difficult for the virtual marks to be fashioned.

The second test followed the majority of the printed material identified with a compartment of blooms moving from the Port of Mombasa, in Kenya, to Rotterdam, in the Netherlands. As the two preliminaries went well, Maersk lined up by rear compartments with pineapples from Colombia, and mandarin oranges from California.

2. Like most dealers, Wal-Mart battles to distinguish and expel nourishment that should be reviewed. At the point when a client turns out to be sick, it can take a long time to recognize the item, shipment, and merchant. To cure this, it reported a year ago that it would begin utilizing blockchain to record and log the starting points of delivering - vital information from a single receipt, including providers, subtle elements on how and where sustenance was developed and who examined it. The database stretches out data from the bed to the individual bundle.

This enables it to promptly discover where a polluted item originated from in a matter of minutes versus days, and besides catch other imperative credits to settle on an educated choice around nourishment stream.

Wal-Mart, has officially finished two test cases programs - moving pork from Chinese ranches to Chinese stores, and deliver from Latin America to the United States - and is currently sure a completed adaptation can be assembled inside a couple of years.

3. BHP depends on merchants at almost every phase in the mining procedure, contracting with geologists and transportation organizations to gather tests and direct examinations that drive business choices including various gatherings circulated crosswise over landmasses. Those merchants regularly monitor shake and liquid examples and investigations with messages and spreadsheets. A lost record can cause vast and costly migraines since the examples enable the organization to choose where to penetrate new wells.

BHP's answer, which began for the current year, is utilized blockchain to record developments of wellbore shake and liquid examples and better secure the constant information that is created amid conveyance. The decentralized record is stockpiling, multi-party information procurement and permanence and besides, quick availability is for the most part angles that will improve its production network.

BHP has now required its sellers to utilize an application to gather live information - with a dashboard and choices on what to do that are exceptionally streamlined to their particular occupations. A specialist taking an example can join information, for example, accumulation time, a lab analyst can include reports, and all will be promptly notified to everybody who approaches. Not any more lost cases or frenzied messages. While individual components of the procedure are the same, the new framework is relied upon to drive inward efficiencies while enabling BHP to work all the more adequately with its accomplices.

Until further notice, in most first arrangements, blockchain is running parallel with organizations' present frameworks - frequently more established databases or spreadsheets like Microsoft's Excel. The hardest part will be to make new plans of action. Conveying blockchain undertaking wide means organizations will frequently need to scrap their current business procedures and begin without any preparation. A company not for the cowardly.

WHY IS THE BLOCKCHAIN TECHNOLOGY IMPORTANT?

Suppose that another innovation is created that could enable numerous gatherings to execute a land bargain. The groups get together and finish the insights about planning, extraordinary conditions and financing. In what manner will these gatherings know they can confide in one another? They would need to confirm their concurrence with outsiders - banks, right groups, government enlistment et cetera. This acquires them starting over from the beginning terms of utilizing the innovation to spare expenses.

In the following stage, the outsiders are currently welcomed to join the land bargain and give their info while the exchange is being made continuously. This lessens the job of the agent essentially. If the arrangement is this straightforward, the mediator can even be wiped out at times. The legal advisors are there to avoid miscommunication and claims. On the off chance that the terms are uncovered forthright, these dangers are significantly diminished. If the financing courses of action are anchored forthright, it will be known ahead of time that the arrangement will be paid for and the gatherings will respect their installments. This conveys us to the last phase of the precedent. On the off chance that the terms of the arrangement and the game plans have been finished, by what means will the method be paid for? The unit of measure would be cash issued by a national bank, which implies managing the banks by and by. Should this occur, the banks would not enable these arrangements to be finished without some due ingenuity on their end, and this would infer costs and deferrals. Is the innovation that helpful in making productivity as yet? It isn't likely.

What is the arrangement? Make advanced money that isn't just barely as straightforward as the give itself, however, is in certainty part of the terms of the agreement. On the off chance that this money is exchangeable with monetary standards issued by national banks, the first necessity remaining is to change over the advanced cash into notable cash like the Canadian dollar or the U.S. dollar which should be possible whenever.

The innovation being suggested in the model is the blockchain innovation. The exchange is the foundation of the economy. A key motivation behind why cash exists is with the end goal of trade. Exchange establishes a high level of action, generation, and charges for different districts. Any reserve funds here that can be connected over the world would be exceptionally noteworthy. For instance, take a gander at facilitated commerce. Before organized business, nations would import and fare with different countries, yet they had an expense framework that would assess imports to limit the impact that outside products had on the neighborhood nation. After unhindered commerce, these expenses were disposed of, and numerous more products were delivered. Indeed, even a little change in exchange rules mostly affected the world's business. The word exchange can be separated into more particular regions like delivery, land, import/fare, and framework and it is clearer how lucrative the blockchain is whether it can spare even a little level of expenses in these regions.

HOW BITCOIN COULD MAKE ASSET MANAGERS OF US ALL

So what is the straight chain and for what reason are you all getting energized?

The square chain is an online decentralized, open record of every single computerized exchange that has occurred. It is electronic cash's likeness a high road bank's history that records transactions between two gatherings.

Similarly, as our cutting-edge managing an accounting framework couldn't work without the way to record the trades of fiat money between people, so too could a computerized arrange not work without the assumption that originates from the capacity to precise document the trading of advanced cash between parties.

It is decentralized as in, not at all like a conventional bank which is the sole holder of an electronic ace record of its record holder's funds the square chain record is shared among all individuals from the system and isn't liable to the terms and states of a specific budgetary establishment or nation.

What of it? For what reason is this desirable over our present managing an accounting framework?

A decentralized money related system guarantees that by sitting outside of the evermore associated current monetary foundation, one can relieve the dangers of being a piece of it when things turn out badly. The three principle hazards of a unified money related framework that were featured because of the 2008 budgetary emergency are credit, liquidity and operational disappointment. In the only us since 2008, there have been 504 bank disappointments because of indebtedness, there being 157 out of 2010 alone. Commonly such a crumble does not endanger account holder's reserve funds because of government/national sponsorship and protection for the initial couple of hundred thousand dollars/pounds, the banks resources for the most part being consumed by another money-related foundation yet the effect of the fall can cause vulnerability and here and now issues with getting to reserves. Since a decentralized framework like the Bitcoin arrange isn't subject to a bank to encourage the exchange of assets between 2 parties yet somewhat depends on its a considerable number of clients to approve transfers it is stronger to such disappointments, it had the same amount of reinforcements as there are individuals from the system to guarantee exchanges keep on being accepted in case of one individual from the system 'crumbling' (see beneath).

A bank requires not bomb anyway to effect on savers, operational I.T. disappointments, for example, those that as of late ceased RBS and Lloyds' clients getting to their records for a considerable length of time can affect on one's capacity to pull back investment funds, these being an aftereffect of a 30-multi-year old inheritance I.T. foundation that is moaning under the strain of staying aware of the development of client spending and an absence of interest all in all. A decentralized framework isn't dependent on this sort of foundation, it instead of being found on the consolidated preparing intensity of its countless clients which guarantees the capacity to scale up as essential, blame in any piece of the framework not making the system come to a standstill.

Liquidity is a last genuine danger of unified frameworks, in 2001 Argentine banks solidified records and presented capital controls because of their obligation emergency, Spanish banks in 2012 changed their little print to enable them to square withdrawals over a specific sum and Cypriot banks quickly solidified client accounts and utilized around 10% of person's investment funds to allow the payment to off the National Debt.

A business analyst at the Peterson Institute for International Economics told the New York Times on the Cypriot model, "What the arrangement reflects is that being an unbound or even anchored investor in euro territory banks isn't as sheltered as it used to be." In a decentralized framework, installment happens without a bank encouraging and approving the exchange, chapters just being supported by the system where there are sufficient assets, there being no outsider to stop trade, misuse it or degrade the sum one holds.

Alright. You make a point. All in all, how does the square chain work?

At the point when an individual makes an advanced exchange, paying another client 1 Bitcoin for instance, a message included 3 segments is created; a reference to a record of data demonstrating the purchaser has the assets to make the installment, the location of the computerized wallet of the beneficiary into which the payment will be made and the sum to pay. Any conditions on the exchange that the purchaser may set are at last included, and the message is 'stamped' with the purchaser's advanced mark.

The computerized mark is involved an open and a private 'key' or code, the message is encoded consequently with the private 'key' and after that sent to the system for the check, just the purchaser's open key having the capacity to decode the message.

This check procedure is intended to guarantee that the destabilizing impact of 'twofold spend' which is a hazard in advanced money systems does not happen. Twofold spend is the place John gives George £1 and after that proceeds to provide Ringo indistinguishable £1 from well (Paul hasn't expected to acquire £1 for a couple of years). This may appear to be equal with our present managing an accounting framework and for sure, the physical demonstration of a trade of fiat money stops John giving without end the same £1 twice however when leading advanced monetary standards which are minor information and where there exists the capacity to duplicate or alter data moderately effortlessly, the danger of 1 unit of computerized cash being cloned and used to make numerous 1 Bitcoin installments is a genuine one. The capacity to do this would demolish any trust in the system and render it useless.

"What the arrangement reflects is that being an unbound or even anchored contributor in euro-region banks isn't as sheltered as it used to be."

To guarantee the framework isn't manhandled the system takes each message consequently made by a purchaser and consolidates a few of these into a 'square' and exhibits them to organize volunteers or 'diggers' to check. Mineworkers contend with one another to be the first to approve a square's legitimacy, master programming on home PCs naturally looking to confirm advanced marks and guarantee that the parts of an exchange message legitimately spill out of the one going before it that was utilized in its creation and that it thus mirrors the square going before it that was utilized in its creation et cetera. Should the entirety of the first parts of a square not equivalent the entire then it is likely that an unintended change was made to a square and it tends to be ceased from being approved. A run of the mill square takes 10 minutes to approve and along these lines for an exchange to experience however this can be accelerated by the purchaser including a little 'tip' to urge mineworkers to approve their demand all the more rapidly, the digger settling the square 'astound' being remunerated with 25 Bitcoins in addition to any 'tips', in this manner is new cash discharged into flow, this boost guaranteeing that volunteers keep on keeping up the system's honesty.

By enabling anybody to check a proposed change against the record and approve it, the square chain expels the requirement for a focal specialist like a bank to deal with this. By dismissing this mediator from the condition a large group of reserve funds as far as endorsed exchange charges, handling times and points of confinement on how much and to whom an exchange can be made can be invalidated.

Sounds too high to be valid.

It is, each sort of framework has its specific dangers, a decentralized one being the same. The fundamental risk to Bitcoin's decentralized system is the '51% danger', 51% alluding to the measure of the system's aggregate excavators working cooperatively in a mining 'pool' to approve exchanges. Because of it winding up more expensive as far as time and handling power for a person to effectively approve an exchange because of the system getting to be greater and more develop singular diggers are presently joining 'pools' where they consolidate their preparing capacity to guarantee a little, however, more normal and predictable return. In principle, should a pool develop sufficiently extensive to contain at least 51% of aggregate system clients it would be able to approve huge twofold spend exchanges or decline to approve valid exchanges end mass, successfully decimating trust in the system? While there is more motivator incorporated with the framework to legally mine Bitcoin than demolish it through extortion the 51% danger speaks to a hazard to such a decentralized framework. To date mining pools are adopting a mindful strategy to this issue and willful advances are being taken to confine imposing business models shaping, it being to everybody's most significant advantage to keep up a steady framework that can be trusted.

So... regardless of this hazard, the Bank of England enjoys the thing that sounds like it could make them bankrupt?

The BoE is looking past Bitcoin and advanced cash installments mainly and imagining ways that the square chain can make existing monetary items and stages more proficient and increase the value of them. One needs to take a gander at existing money related resources, for example, stocks, credits or subordinates which areas of now digitized yet which sit on incorporated systems to welcome the open doors that exist for the person by expelling the broker...

... What's more, turning into your stockbroker. Shaded Coin is an undertaking that intends to enable anybody to transform any of their advantages or property into something they can exchange. Think 'The Antiques Roadshow.' I cherish that show, particularly when a dear find that she's been utilizing a fourteenth Century Ming dish worth £200,000 to keep the organic product in on her sideboard. Hued Coins would permit the proprietor of the meal (or their auto or house) to have at least one of their Bitcoins speak to a section or entire of the estimation of their advantage so they could be exchanged trade for different merchandise and enterprises, a solitary Bitcoin holding an estimate of the whole £200,000 or they issuing 200 coins each with a view of £1000.

Correspondingly, a business could issue shares spoken to by electronic money straightforwardly to general society which could thus at that point be exchanged without the requirement for a costly IPO, or joint stock traders and investors could vote to utilize a protected framework like how exchange messages are as of now made. Patrick Byrne, CEO of one of the US's most prominent retailers which were the first major online retailer to acknowledge worldwide Bitcoin installments is as of now investigating intends to make such a stock trade fueled by the square chain which he expectations will nullify current intrinsic issues, for example, 'injurious exposed short offering' where brokers can offer offers they don't claim which drives down provide costs and which was felt added to the fall of Lehman Brothers.

The digitizing of advantages could likewise upset the crowdfunding business. Kickstarter is a case of a stage that encourages the financing of items by miniaturized scale installments from intrigued individuals, regularly as a byproduct of little endless supply of the venture, for example, marked stock or a duplicate of one of the principal items to be created. With the capacity to effectively digitize a benefit and issue partakes in it and every future interest for instance speculators might be more disposed to contribute all the more vigorously.

What's more, talking about crowdfunding... Vitalik Buterin as of late brought £15m up in swarm sourced subsidizing for his Ethereum Project which he accepts will speak to the eventual fate of the square chain. The task bolsters various programming dialects to enable designers to construct online items and administrations like web-based life, hunt or talk discussions as options in contrast to those kept running by partnerships like Google, Facebook, and Twitter. "You can compose anything that you would have the capacity to compose on a server and put it on to the blockchain," Buterin told Wired. "Rather than JavaScript making calls to the server, you would make calls to the blockchain." Currently, a network of 200 clients is building voting applications, space name enlistment centers, swarm sourcing stages, and PC amusements to keep running on Ethereum, 'ethers' mined through the upkeep of the scene by volunteers being required for this.

The capability of the square tie to enhance the manner in which we convey, bank, deal with our advantages and so on is gigantic and just restricted by the creative energy of individuals like Vitalik Buterin and the Ethereum people group and the ability of current organizations to change.

7 BLOCKCHAIN APPLICATION IDEAS THAT HELP IN BUSINESS

1. Payments and Money Transfers

Perhaps the most well-known blockchain application is being able to send and receive payments. Since blockchain technology has its beginnings in cryptocurrency, this makes sense. But, how exactly is this beneficial for small business owners.

By using blockchain technology, you're able to transfer funds directly and securely to anyone you want in the world almost instantly and at ultra-low fees. That's because there aren't any intermediaries slowing down the transfer of funds between several banks and charging outrageous transaction fees.

This practice is especially useful if you have remote employees or are involved in the global marketplace.

Companies like Abra, Bitwage, and Coinpip are leading the charge in using the blockchain to transfer funds or handle payroll.

2. Smart Contracts

Believe it or not, the term "smart contract"' has been in-use since 1993, but now it's associated with the blockchain thanks to the emergence of 2013's the Ethereum Project.

This Project "is a decentralized platform that runs smart contracts: applications that run exactly as programmed without any possibility of downtime, censorship, fraud or third party interference."

"Smart contracts" are "self-automated computer programs that can carry out the terms of any contract," writes Chris DeRose in American Banker. In a nutshell "it is a financial security held in escrow by a network that is routed to recipients based on future events, and computer code."

With "smart contracts" businesses will be able to bypass regulations and "lower the costs for a subset of our most common financial transactions." Additionally, these contracts will be unbreakable.

Companies like Slock, which is an Ethereum-enabled internet-of-things platform, is already using this application so that customers can rent anything from bicycles to apartments by unlocking a smart lock after both parties agreed on the terms of the contract.

Furthermore, global banks are using "smart contracts" to improve the syndicated loan market. One such company that is using blockchains to issue microloans is Synaps.

3. Notary

Blockchain technology can also be used as a convenient and inexpensive notary service. For instance, apps like Uproov, which is a smartphone multimedia platform, can be notarized instantly after a user creates an image, video, or sound recording.

Meanwhile, stampd.io, can actually be used to notarize proof of ownership of digital creation.

4. Distributed Cloud Storage

Distributed cloud storage will be another blockchain application that businesses can take advantage of. Storj, company that's using the blockchain to provide users with affordable, fast, and secure cloud storage.

VentureBeat Storj founder Shawn Wilkinson said that, "Simply using excess hard drive space, users could store the traditional cloud 300 times over," much like how you can rent out a room on Airbnb. Wilkinson added, "Considering the world spends $22 billion + on cloud storage alone, this could open a revenue stream for average users, while significantly reducing the cost to store data for companies and personal users."

This makes distributed cloud storage one of the more interesting blockchain applications — and one for small businesses to keep an eye on.

5. Digital Identity

Did you know that fraud is estimated to cost the industry around $18.5 billion annually? In other words, that means that for every $3 spent, $1 is going to ad fraud. Because of that, security is a top concern for businesses of all sizes who want to utilize the blockchain wallet.

"Blockchain technologies make tracking and managing digital identities both secure and efficient, resulting in seamless sign-on and reduced fraud.

"Blockchain technology offers a solution to many digital identity issues, where identity can be uniquely authenticated in an irrefutable, immutable, and secure manner," says Rosic. "Current methods use problematic password-based systems of shared secrets exchanged and stored on insecure systems. Blockchain-based authentication systems are based on irrefutable identity verification using digital signatures based on public key cryptography."

With blockchain identity authentication, "the only check performed is whether or not the transaction was signed by the correct private key. It is inferred that whoever has access to the private key is the owner and the exact identity of the owner is deemed irrelevant."

Blockchain technology can be applied to identity applications in areas like IDs, online account login, E-Residency, passports, and birth certificates.

Companies such as ShoCard are using the blockchain to validate an individual's identity on their mobile device.

6. Supply-Chain Communications & Proof-of-Provenance

"Most of the things we buy aren't made by a single entity, but by a chain of suppliers who sell their components (e.g., graphite for pencils) to a company that assembles and markets the final product.

The problem with this system is that if one of these components fails "the brand takes the brunt of the backlash," says Phil Gomes of Edelman Digital.

By utilizing blockchain technology "a company could proactively provide digitally permanent, auditable records that show stakeholders the state of the product at each value-added step."

Provenance and SkuChain are just two examples of companies attempting resolve this issue.

7. Gift Cards and Loyalty Programs

The blockchain could also assist retailers that offer gift cards, loyalty programs, and other digital assets by making the process cheaper and more secure by cutting out the middlemen and using the blockchain's unique verification capabilities.

Gyft Block, which is a partnership between Gyft and bitcoin API developer Chain, issues digital gift card that can be securely traded on the blockchain's public ledger.

CHAPTER THREE

CRYPTOGRAPHY AND NETWORK SECURITY

A move of information in a business framework regularly happens with the assistance of the digital medium. In such situation security of this information stays at the prime focal point of the considerable number of associations. Cryptography here assumes a critical job in keeping up the protection of the exchanged data. Give us a chance to investigate the all through this procedure of center significance.

What is cryptography?

Cryptography is the strategy to conceal the data with the utilization of microdots, picture word blending, or with some different ways. In the specialized field, it tends to be named as scrambling plain content into an encoded frame, more often than not called Ciphertext, on the other hand, to change over it into decoded arrange known as Clear text. This procedure of encoding and deciphering is called cryptography and individuals honing this field are known as cryptographers.

What are the Objectives of Cryptography?

Current cryptography takes after the beneath targets.

1. Secrecy any individual who is out of the circle can't comprehend the data between the sender and beneficiary.

2. Uprightness no modification is conceivable once the message is discharged.

3. Verification data and sources in the cryptography framework are valid. Both sender and beneficiary can distinguish one another and starting point or goal of the data.

4. Non-disavowal none of the sender or collectors can venture back of the message at a later stage.

5. Access control-just approved individuals can get to the secret information.

To satisfy the above destinations, the accompanying organizations of cryptography are honed.

1. Symmetric cryptography-otherwise called mystery key cryptography; it is a strategy in which both sender and beneficiary offer a similar mystery code and key for encryption and decoding. This procedure is valuable on the off chance that you are speaking with a set number of individuals, in any case, it isn't much help for mass correspondence.

2. Topsy-turvy cryptography-this is otherwise called crucial open cryptography in which, isolated keys are utilized for encryption and unscrambling. This is helpful for essential trade and computerized marks, for example, RSA, advanced mark calculation, open essential cryptography standard and so on.

3. Message-process in this, a hash work is utilized to for all time scramble the information. This is additionally called one-way encryption.

Cryptography ensures the system assets against change, demolition, and their unapproved utilize. They secure the system framework, IT resources, and the secret information. In the present situation, it has turned out to be very simple to modify or limit the information and data. Robbery of classified data is again a discomforting marvel.

We at I Global help you to get the understanding of exceptionally essential and all-inclusive honed cryptographic methods. We give you careful learning of system security framework and related instruments.

CRYPTOGRAPHY - TYPES OF CRYPTOGRAPHY

Cryptographic strategies have been being used since the season of the Sumerians (3500 BCE). Cryptography depends on mystery keys, which, as you'll review, are the contribution to the calculation that delivers the figure content. There are two essential kinds of cryptography: customary cryptography and crucial open cryptography. In conventional cryptography, a single key is utilized to perform both encryption and decoding. Since the keys are indistinguishable, they're alluded to as symmetric keys. Since just a unique core is used in conventional cryptography, it's less secure. On the off chance that somebody other than the planned beneficiary finds the key, he can decode the first message. Another downside to conventional cryptography is that it's hazardous to convey. If somebody blocks the key on its way to the expected beneficiary, the security of the message is imperiled. PGP Desktop additionally enables you to scramble singular records and envelopes, a segment of your hard plate assigned as a virtual circle, or your whole hard plate.

In broad daylight key cryptography, two unmistakable keys are utilized an open core to perform encryption and a private key to perform unscrambling. Since the keys are unique, they're alluded to as Hitler kilter keys. This enables anybody to scramble a message yet just people with the relating private key to decode words. To illuminate, how about we take a gander at a model. If Paul needs to make an impression on Sara, he utilizes Sara's open key to encode the message. At the point when Sara gets the message, she uses her private key to unscramble it. For whatever length of time that every individual in the message circle keeps his/her private key completely closed, just the expected beneficiary can decode the message. Open cryptography likewise defeats the dispersion issue because only available keys should be sent over the uncertain system; private keys are looked after locally.

Next, how about we direct our concentration toward a functional case of crucial open cryptography. In the accompanying areas, we'll utilize an example application, PGP Desktop, to demonstrate to you best practices to create a public/private key combine to anchor both email and texts. We'll additionally show to you industry standards to distribute your open key to the PGP Global Directory so others can send encoded messages to you. At the point when your machine returns on the web, the PGP Setup Assistant dispatches naturally. This utility causes you to finish an underlying setup, including creating another critical combine and alternatively distributing your open key to the PGP Global Directory. Note that you should complete the PGP Setup Assistant undertakings before utilizing the essential application itself. Since PGP is introduced for all clients as a matter of course, you have to empower it for every window account exclusively. This implies you have to sign in with the fitting Windows record initially and afterward allow PGP for the dynamic record.

PC CRYPTOGRAPHY

Cryptography is the exploration of changing messages to make them secure and safe to assault. The strict significance of cryptography is "mystery composing." On the off chance that the first message is sent through a system, at that point any programmer can get access and change its importance. To guarantee the security of the word, the first message is altered to cipher text utilizing an encryption calculation by the sender. What's more, the recipient uses a decoding calculation to transform the ciphertext once more into plaintext.

Encryption and unscrambling calculations are called figures. Also, those calculations work on an arrangement of numbers called Key. To scramble a message, we require an encryption calculation, encryption key, and the open content. These make the ciphertext. Thus to unscramble a word, we need a decoding calculation, unscrambling key and the ciphertext. These uncover the plaintext. In cryptography, three characters (Alice, Bob, and Eve) are exceptionally well known. Alice is the individual who sends the message and Bob is the beneficiary. Eve exasperates this correspondence by blocking signal to reveal the information.

There are two sorts of figures (cryptography calculations)

1-Symmetric-key or Secret Key Cryptography

2-Asymmetric-key or Public-key Cryptography

Symmetric-Key Cryptography

In Symmetric-Key Cryptography, a similar key is utilized by both sender and collector. So the key must be known to the two gatherings. The customary figures are substitution figure and transposition figure. A substitution figure substitutes one image with another. For instance, we can supplant character B with G and F with X. In a transposition figure, an area of a character is changed in the cipher text. We should talk about some essential symmetric data.

DES (Data Encryption Standard) - DES is a symmetric-key square figure planned by IBM. A square figure isolates the plaintext into squares and uses a similar key to encode and decode the squares. DES encrypts a 64-bit plaintext square utilizing a 64-bit key. It is broadly used in military, aviation and knowledge foundations on account of its quick task and security.

Triple DES - It is progressed from DES since three keys are utilized in progression to scramble a message. It has likewise expanded the critical size to 112 bits.

AES (Advanced Encryption Standard) - AES is an exceptionally complex round figure with three different key sizes: 128, 192, or 156 bits.

Thought (International Data Encryption Algorithm) - Xuejia Lai and James Massey created it. The square size is 64 bits, and the critical dimension is 128 bits.

Blowfish -Bruce Schneier produced it. The square size is 64 and critical dimension somewhere in the range of 32 and 448.

CAST-128 - It was produced via Carlisle Adams and Stafford Tavares. The square size is 64 bits, and the critical dimension is 128 bits.

RC5 - Ron Rivest planned RC5. It has a unique square size and key sizes.

Hilter kilter Key Cryptography

This uses two keys: a private key and an open key. The public key is utilized to scramble to message through private key is used to decode. People in general encryption key is made accessible to whoever needs to use it, yet the private key is kept mystery by the critical proprietor. The procedure is clarified underneath:

- If A needs to make an impression on B, the message is encoded by a utilizing B's open key.

- If B gets the message, the message is decoded by utilizing B's private key. No other beneficiary can unscramble the word.

RSA - It is most ordinarily utilized basic open calculation. It is named by its designer's name Rivest, Shamir, and Adelman (RSA). It uses two numbers as the general population and private keys. RSA is helpful for short messages and utilized furthermore in excellent marks. In any case, it is moderate if the message measure is long.

WEAKNESS OF CRYPTOGRAPHY

Cryptography is a conventional technique for ensuring the delicate data yet it is not the slightest bit an idiot-proof strategy. The inquiry isn't about the programmers or other individuals breaking into the code misguidedly again there are times when such individuals require not to break into the system to get the mystery data. Or maybe, they need to sit tight for the opportune time and strike at the correct time as the data isn't scrambled continuously. It might be hard to envision such circumstance however it is very straightforward.

Cryptography can shroud the data if it is scrambled and the span until it remains encoded. Be that as it may, the mystery data, for the most part, does not begin out as struggled. There is regularly a period amid which the mystery data is secured and not ensured. This period is the most open time for the classified data. Additionally, the mystery data or any encoded information is by and large not utilized in the scrambled frame. Anyway, secret the data is, it should be decoded before being made usable. So it is again outside the cryptographic envelope each time it is to be utilized. Therefore, the purported encoded data can be effectively gotten to amid this period and can be effortlessly obtained and used by the individual who isn't qualified for doing as such.

There are numerous examples where cryptography can demonstrate value and have substantiated itself and yet it is powerless in specific circumstances. There are two measurements into this. The first is its inadequacy sequestered from everything or scrambling certain things, and the other is its futility against securing certain sorts of assaults or dangers.

Discussing the initial measurement, i.e., inadequacy sequestered from everything or scrambling certain things, we have:

1. Physical stash - No one can encode the real booty. Although they can be covered up inside some bundle or holder, they can't be encrypted and made pointless to the average mass or prying eyes of the security offices.

2. Money - We all convey trade out the physical shape and also virtual frame using plastic cash. Both the sorts can't be scrambled. To the extent virtual money is concerned, the method for getting to it must be climbed and not merely the money. If the individual figures out how to break the virtual money account, the money will be gone.

3. Physical gatherings and preparing - Secret conferences or instructional meetings of security organizations or any ill-conceived office can't be encoded to make it invisible. The ideal path is to direct these gatherings in an undisclosed area.

Also, cryptography is of no assistance to encode development of a man or anything to and from a specific area, the activities related to it or the way of life of the individual. If a man or office watches out for such individual or his developments, the day by day schedule and the encompassing of the individual can be conclusively known.

Taking a gander at the second measurement, i.e., the pointlessness of cryptography against ensuring certain sorts of assaults or dangers, we profit any security using cryptography against:

1. Witnesses

2. Covert spying

3. Bugs

4. Photographic proof

5. Declaration

It is a sheer wastage of time to imagine that cryptography alone can give excellent security against any sorts of dangers which include spillage of secret data. Cryptography, not the slightest bit is an obvious security check. The regions in which it gives security are not all anchored and can be endangered. Cryptography is just a little piece of the assurance required for excellent protection.

CRYPTOGRAPHY - TYPES AND ADVANTAGES OF CRYPTOGRAPHY

The least rigorous definition accessible concerning, what cryptography is that it is the investigation of utilizing science to encode and unscramble data, which implies putting into or unraveling from a numerical dialect. What are the approaches to use this innovation and realize what preferences are? Along these lines, as should be obvious, this appears as if cryptography would be exceptionally troublesome. By the by, this is essential because everything on your PC is put away in cryptography.

Cryptography turns out to be significantly more unpredictable, however. This is because people perceive numbers as digits from 0 to 9, yet your PC can see 0 and 1. In that capacity, this double framework utilizes bits rather than fingers. With a specific end goal to change over bits to digits you should duplicate the number of bits by 0.3. This will at that point give you a decent estimation of a big motivator for it.

Presently some different definitions are essential to comprehend here. To begin with, you ought to understand that a savage power assault is a point at which the majority of the conceivable blends of numbers are utilized to either decode or scramble materials. Furthermore, a word reference assault happens at whatever point a man a go at using all conceivable has known passwords, which is shockingly a little sum, to frame a charge. There are a few people, for example, the administration, who might benefit from knowing cryptography and are hence known as an enemy. Then again, the individuals who ought not to help from this entrance are known as a critical lumberjack.

The majority of this presumably still sounds exceptionally hard to get it. This is the reason it takes so much instruction on the off chance that you need to function as a cryptographer. There are just a few people who can genuinely see the majority of this and along these lines utilize it to help the majority of whatever remains of us with our day by day PC needs. It is additionally why the general population who work in this field profit doing as such.

For what reason do you require cryptosystems, Government, privately owned businesses and colleges trade information over the Internet with their confided in accomplices? They need a full secure information trade; no programmer or outsider ought to have the capacity to catch the critical information. To overcome security, mystery, and significance of data being hacked or stolen, cryptography gives two sorts of cryptosystems.

First is "Symmetric" framework under, which cryptosystems utilize a similar mystery key to scramble or decode a message got information parcel from confided in accomplices.

The other cryptosystem is the topsy-turvy framework under, which two unique keys are utilized to encode and unscramble the message or got information parcel. On open core is used to encrypt the information or message and the private key on accepting end are utilized to decode the signal or information parcel.

Presently the inquiry is how we would send these keys to confide in accomplices. Other than most new apparatuses utilized in checking, anchoring information trade, keys are gone through admitted in messengers to maintain a strategic distance from information being blocked by programmers.

Encryption - "is a procedure of changing or changing over ordinary content or information data into jabber content."

Decoding - "is a procedure of changing or changing over rubbish message back to rectify message or information by utilizing encryption strategy."

Social Cryptography

We have heard various types of encryption in light of different scientific figuring's, prime numbers, factorizations, yet limitless bodies progressively looked with the loose faith in regards to PC researchers and mathematicians in their day by day work, as much as science dependably has a flawless hole or a period for such encryption be broken and naturally making them out of date.

As we as a whole know the encryption is just systematizing something that is out in the open comprehension, in which all may know or approach with no earlier learning, yet with the appearance of PC innovation in our life, everything turned out to be very numerical, mostly in light of the fact that our PCs just perceive the paired 0 and 1, and in this way numerous specialists have made some extremely intriguing approaches to scramble data utilizing scientific capacities after some time.

As we as a whole know, each day that passes builds the figuring power so gigantic, making every day need to create new types of encryption or exponential development of keys to contain such event, on the off chance that we a reasonable prospect of exponential growth of computational power for a considerable length of time to come, why we are squandering our opportunity of creating workarounds, which will be out of date in a brief span? Why make calculations astounding, with numerical structures are never utilized in 10 years a solitary processor of a work area of our kids and grandkids will break effortlessly? So accept this open the door to talk somewhat more than an idea at no other time tended to the concept of cryptography Behavior.

Encryption Behavior does not absolve the utilization of innovation nor the figuring power, yet has one unique distinction with the encryption given numerical inquiries, it utilizes the registering authority to approve the procedure included in light of social parts of the person using the same.

Abridging the conduct Encryption depends on a perpetual cycle of work as beneath advice

Learning of the individual => Creating profile cryptographic framework PC => Improvement of the profile cryptographic human => Knowledge of Individual vastly.

A decent case of utilizing a login utilizing the encryption conduct would be an application in which the User with restricted access to the working framework for a specific time and it would use its instruments, access to site pages, impart by means of texting and through recorded arrangement of such access would make a profile cryptographic this individual, and consistently would refine the profile achieving a level of information through the PC framework that would make the character of the individual approaching this framework. What's more, this idea is just conceivable with the coming of Web 2.0 where we have working frameworks logs in view of the Internet (cloud) thus the profile would not have the movability issue on various PCs, basically get to the Internet, and the working framework in the cloud would make any User Authentication.

The idea to make no issues of unapproved access to the framework time to decide whether that individual meets or not the necessities of the profile, would approach do modules in which this individual would contact confined at first and winning hits throughout his utilization and validation

COMPUTERS AND CRYPTOGRAPHY

PCs have changed cryptography. Before the PC age, cryptography was just used to encode messages. When PCs began to be utilized in cryptography, propelled, science turned out to be imperative to make robust encryption. PCs and the Internet have additionally extended cryptography to incorporate verification and excellent marks.

PC encryption can be separated into two classes, symmetric encryption and deviated encryption. Symmetric encryption is additionally called single-key encryption because a similar key is utilized to both scramble and decode the message. Topsy-turvy encryption uses two unique keys, one private key, and one open key. Topsy-turvy encoding is frequently called public key cryptography.

Symmetric encryption can be made exceptionally secure and quick. The principle downside with symmetric encryption is the critical appropriation. Before symmetric encryption can be utilized, the key must be safely disseminated to all gatherings. This rapidly turns into a calculated lousy dream when the number of individuals included increments. The key ought to likewise be changed frequently to limit the danger of utilizing a key that has been imperiled. For encryption on the Internet, symmetric encryption is certifiably not an available alternative. This isn't just because of the broad measure of keys that would be required yet additionally because before you can begin discussing safely with somebody, you have to concur on a mystery key.

Hilter kilter encryption usually is slower than symmetric encryption however it is substantially more reasonable for the Internet. Crucial secure dispersion isn't an issue; all gatherings have one private key and one open key. The proprietor knows the private key; the comparing key then again is known by everybody.

The private and open keys are scientifically related, if a message has been encoded with somebody's private key, just the comparing open key can unscramble the content. This implies you can make sure that the proprietor of the private key encoded the message. Furthermore, you can encrypt a message utilizing somebody's open key and send the message over unreliable ways. Since nobody aside from the proprietor of the comparing private key can decode the signal, it doesn't make a difference if others get hold of the scrambled content. This likewise implies you are guaranteed that you are speaking with the individual who is the proprietor of the private key.

How might you make sure that you have the correct open key? Somebody could give you a phony crucial and disclose to you that it is the public key of your bank. On the off chance that you choose to acknowledge the key, you could wind up giving the entirety of your keeping money and MasterCard subtle elements to the sham endlessly. The arrangement is straightforward; Internet programs have various preloaded testament experts that they will trust. These declaration specialists issue authentications that demonstrate that a site is hugely the site it professes to be. If a place has an authentication issued by a testament specialist your program does not confide in you will get a notice saying that a divulged in endorsement expert did not release the declaration.

AN INTRODUCTION TO CRYPTOGRAPHY

Present day security can influence individuals to end up more strained than it gives a sentiment of security. A large number of clients sign on to the web ordinary and safety is a factor typical to all. Electronic installments, E-business are a few angles embraced today through the web. Each passing minute some measure of information is exchanged between two gatherings that will heap up to an enormous amount of information when we consider the number of individuals was conveying through the web all around the globe. The information being shared two gatherings is in a perfect world implied for nobody other than the two concerned meetings and thus the need to share information through a safe way is required. Cryptography can be called as one such piece of conveying securely.

Cryptography is said to be old artistry and is characterized as the art of composing or conveying through mystery codes. It is trusted that cryptography has been in presence from as far back as 1900 B.C even though a couple of specialist's rally behind the point that cryptography appeared just some time in the wake of composing was created. With the continual development in present-day innovation, it was just inescapable that cutting-edge types of cryptography would be put into impact. In the field of media communications, cryptography is fundamental amid the procedure of correspondence over an unbound medium or system particularly the web which is utilized everywhere throughout the world. Cryptography is used for the sheltered entry of communication in the littlest to the most significant systems as one needs to guarantee to satisfy every one of the necessities that comprise a protected and secure connection.

Some essential security plans are required during the time spent correspondence between a sender and a recipient.

1. Verification: Authentication essentially intends to set up one's personality. In the present situation, most host to have validation procedures on the web are for the most part name based and address based. Be that as it may, both these systems are incredibly feeble from a security perspective.

2. Keeping up security and privacy: Whatever message is being passed on by the sender should just be perused by the beneficiary and not by an outsider. Data ought not to be spilled.

3. The respectability of message: It must be ensured that the word gotten by the beneficiary has not been altered at all. It ought to be getting in the correct unique frame in which it has been sent.

4. Non-denial: A strategy ought to be set up to decide and check no ifs ands or buts that the sender has without a doubt sent the message.

HOW TO KEEP FILES SECURE? CRYPTOGRAPHY, FILE WIPER, INTERNET PRIVACY

It is understood certainty that documents erased in Windows will be recoverable. So any individual who approaches the PC will have the capacity to undelete record and the substance of the report. It is by all accounts the issue of best mystery associations and organizations. However, truth be told, end-clients likewise should think about this issue.

Journal PC may be stolen or lost. For this situation, the most powerless is data that resembles erased, yet is accessible for covering. Another issue is web movement. Any Internet program leaves a considerable measure of follows, including the connections to visited locales, utilized loggings and at some point secret phrase. This perspective may prompt wholesale fraud issue, when somebody could take a great deal of data about you from your PC, from program treats.

If was attempts to take care of this issue, we ought to comprehend that first, we have to realize what is the wellspring of potential peril and how would we be able to deal with these dangers. I'm sure you are worried about utilizing MasterCard's on the web, yet basic guidelines will utilize your MasterCard's just on confided in sites, and your information won't be stolen. So you continue using your charge card getting advantages of buying on the web.

The main straightforward proposal about remaining secure is: "keep your touchy documents in the secure place." It's not hard now as there exist freeware and open source encryption frameworks, for example, True Crypt. Another methodology is to utilize encryption arrangement of end-client programs, for example, encryption proposed in compress record configuration or word documents. Cryptology calculations there are difficult to split (really, somebody will have the capacity to discover the secret phrase just utilizing original power investigation). On the off chance that you send an excellent record to your partner, employ a secret word assurance for this document or put this record into a secured file.

Speaking with others is a whole secure perspective. If you utilize straightforward encryption frameworks, at that point before conveying you should trade the secret phrase, this may be not extremely helpful, that is the reason it's a superior plan to utilize one-key cryptography.

The second assignment is to ensure that your information is anything but challenging to undelete. Utilize record shredder to anchor erase (wipe document); a better thought is utilizing foundation mode record shredder, which needn't bother with your activity to anchor each erasure. Calendar standard clean, free space task, this isn't generally 100% security, yet it will keep around 98% of beforehand erased information secure. How to pick document shredder to utilize? Download some free or allowed to-attempt undelete programming and check if records wiped with document shredder are recoverable. There may be some other security perspectives, (for example, brief histories), yet for most clients, it's sufficiently very.

The routine inquiry is - what number of passes do I require? The appropriate response is 1-pass overwriting amid wiping is sufficient. Overwriting information Peter Guttmann recommended a few times in 1996. Where solid circles were much slower, little in size and more awful in quality. For these days' plates, this thought isn't generally pertinent and one-pass overwriting is sufficient.

Remaining secure at the web. It's anything but a hard errand, think about introducing the most recent form of internet browser, Firefox is incredible new programming. Consider utilizing a firewall that is incorporated with the framework or is appropriated as a remain single instrument. Try not to pass your information to the sites that you don't trust. Sites that acknowledge MasterCard's must help secure conventions for obtaining pages. Concerning wholesale fraud issue, the quick thought is to peruse more about conceivable courses for meddle to take your information; there is no much programming that may help with this.

At last, my suggestion is: ensure you keep records in secure place and provide it's impractical to discover your documents elsewhere, for example, undelete beforehand erased records. It's basic, yet it's a decent method to remain secure.

So what archives do you have on your PC framework? Money related data, therapeutic records, private email or occasion assessment forms. What data would you be able to bear to offer up to cybercriminals?

In case you're similar to me, at that point the appropriate response is NONE! The unfortunate reality is that a great many people have almost no encryption frameworks at all on their information. On the off chance that that is the situation then you could conceivably be giving without end everything to cybercriminals. So what would you be able to do? Locate a Simple and straightforward to utilize topsy-turvy encryption program is the best place to begin. Without going into the historical backdrop of figure encryption and crucial open cryptography, well take a gander at a few territories we can make a shot at by picking the correct encryption programming. I speculate you're perusing this part since you comprehend that as of now require encryption. In any case, like most, need a little direction on what sort of encryption framework to utilize and the best kind of programming to purchase.

Encryption:

Everybody comprehends that we require encryption somehow, keeping the money, PC, however, most wouldn't know the first spot to begin. Crucial open foundation inshore is a cryptography framework that empowers clients to convey on an unbound open system safely. There are heaps of projects on the web that do encryption. However, most give you a couple of highlights like encoding content and documents. What is required is a program that offers you encoding content and materials, envelopes, producing the key, making declarations and CA's to marking, secure erase, auto essential reinforcement thus one. I think you get the point; an encryption program ought to have more than a couple of things.

When I initially began finding out about encryption, I found that it was so tricky seeing exactly how most encryption programming functioned. Exploring was a bad dream, producing keys you needed to have a super tech degree or Knowledge of direction line and merely doing an essential undertaking was incomprehensible. Presently, after 14 years there are just a bunch of encryption organizations that comprehend the basic is better; an encryption program ought to be proficient yet comfortable to utilize.

Solid Password:

Symmetric encryption programs are secret word based and simple for a great many people to utilize, the issue here is merely the secret key. I can't let you know being an IT proficient exactly how often I've seen exceptionally weak passwords that I observe to be un-genuine. Passwords like: 12345, some portion of SS#, road or house number, feline's name, canine's name, kid's name and even the word secret phrase utilized for the secret word. The issue here is that passwords are too complicated to recall if complex and the short ones are anything but trying to split.

Hilter kilter Encryption:

Hilter kilter encryption programs function admirably because you don't need to stress over passwords or who has your open key. Your public key is for everybody, and the main thing you have to stress over is anchoring your private key. With this sort of cryptology framework, there's no stress over unbound transmission or how to get a secret key to your beneficiary. These keys can be utilized to sign records, message and send them as ASCII in a standard unbound email. Indeed, you can encode an index and post it as ASCII in an email.

Secret word Protected Key Store:

When searching for your encryption program. Search for a program that secret key ensures the principle key store that holds the majority of your open and private keys. Find a program that keeps private keys encoded.

What Type of Key Pair Should I Use?

Most encryption programs utilize RSA and offer a critical size of 1024 through 4096. RSA key size 768 has just been split, and now they're taking a shot at attempting to break 1024. In case you will utilize RSA, I would genuinely prescribe the critical size of 4096. Be that as it may, my last proposal is to use Elliptic Curve Key P-521. This implies finding a program that can create elliptic bend keys; not all OpenPGP programs produce circular bend keys.

Support for X.509 Certificates:

Search for a program that backings X.509 declarations and can produce X.509 endorsements, testament expert (CA), self-marked authentications and ready to change over PFX to PEM design. OpenPGP essentially folds over the testament with the goal that you can utilize this authentication or your endorsement for encryption and unscramble and also marking.

Testament Server:

An encryption program ought to likewise bolster getting keys to and from a testament server. The program ought to have the capacity to look the server for keys, offer central numerous administration to seek and also submit open keys to the server.

FILE ENCRYPTION SOFTWARE - WHY YOU NEED IT

The present world is the universe of fast-moving innovation demonstrating supernatural occurrences for the welfare of humanity. For example, the field of Medical Science is achieving the turning points in sparing one's life and enhancing his/her wellbeing. Thus, the area of Computer Science is continually furnishing person simplicity and solace with most recent improvement and progressive developments.

Out of much headway in the field of Computer Science, one is the utilization of down to earth cryptography. Cryptography is the craft of composing mystery codes. It is a technique for putting away data so that it must be uncovered by those individuals you wish to see it yet conceals this data from all others.

Cryptography is likewise called Encryption. There are numerous reasons for utilizing encryption strategy to secure your classified data like it is a reliable technique, simple to use, straightforward and guarantees finish security. In any case, the most significant test in ensuring information by using an encryption strategy is to follow that information progressing is legitimately encoded.

Thus, you may require a File Encryption Software that would password be able to ensure your information and guarantee finish security for the information moving. There is just a couple of programming that can legitimately encode information progressing, and out of them, you will need the best programming to scramble your data as you would prefer not to bargain on your security. Continuously ensure that you pick programming which provides the protection of your information moving and offers appropriate compactness highlight with which you can convey your data with you anyplace you need.

The best File Encryption Software is the one which offers most extreme security at first, similar to Folder Lock which offers quickest encryption, as well as provides some extra highlights like locking insurance with which you can bolt documents and envelopes and make them secret key ensured, convenience that enables you to convey your information with yourself anyplace you need and guaranteed the most significant security of the information progressing.

The most effective method to Protect Your Privacy and Data

With expanding utilization of advanced databases for putting away the entirety of our records, information insurance is vital for guaranteeing that our most secret data. Entrapped in a trap of frailties and vulnerabilities, it stays basic that we convey the most ideal intends to anchor our private data from the individuals who may benefit or generally try to obliterate our lives for their diversion. In such conditions, the weight of duty does in actuality encroach upon us to face these dangers utilizing all methods available to us.

However, there is just so much we can do to ensure ourselves without utilization of encryption and cryptography in the advanced world, where the torrent of malignancy continually jeopardizes our protection and information. If at any time our prosperity has been more undermined, it is currently. It is for this very reason successful systems to counter these dangers, with proactive measures are utilized to combat, avoid, and perhaps kill the harm sustained by such acts.

The most practical procedure, at a typical, keeps an eye on benefit is the aimless utilization of Data Encryption, especially for all delicate data, which might prompt trade-off of security and prosperity of a person. Undoubtedly, information robbery and break is one of the gravest risk confronting humanity in the 21st century, and without legitimate security conventions, our exceptionally thriving can be discolored hopeless.

Insights progressively manage that PC robberies are on the ascent, as are hacking occurrences everywhere throughout the world. The test which such patterns posture to humankind is considerable, and an intensive procedure to avert probability of such events ought to be based upon vigorous encryption, which is impervious past all methods and techniques. Encryption is our only rescue in this repulsive war and battle against the loss of our security.

Getting to the current circumstance, without adequate responsive measures will deplete our opportunity and assets. The individuals who advocate or limit the seriousness of the risk genuinely do miss the larger picture of what is in question here. Most information and security assurance neglect to actualize and join leap forward strategies. Firewalls, while the compositional base for security plan and technique, can never be sufficient to avoid protection and data rupture, robbery and infringement. Same applies to that smart enemy of infections suites which guarantee to alleviate man from all which debilitate our lives.

Envision, somebody, entering into the firewall, and taking unfortified authoritative and survey information. In our universe of observation and regular information gathering, we are on the edge of a lethal one-two punch. This not just disregards our protection and records our lives, yet besides, uncovered the extensive gathered information to all type of robbery and break. Such occasions must be averted utilizing astute and unbreakable procedure of encryption and cryptography.

Data protector is one of the information assurance programming's like genuine sepulcher they utilize military review computerized vaults to anchor our information, which is perhaps extraordinary compared to other activities so far to secure data on a worldwide scale.

The results can be accursing for every one of us if we neglect to utilize information security systems which adequately position our information past the purpose of burglary and break.

VARIOUS USES OF ELECTRONIC SIGNING

They are to guarantee the genuineness of the report to the recipient. Marks are likewise used to ensure that the record has not been changed at all. Be that as it may, with the appearance of innovation, manually written marks are not an extremely good mean of guaranteeing the legitimacy of an advanced report. For this reason, the idea of web-based Signing was presented.

An internet signing, to be more exact, is an electronic mark used to verify that the substance of the message has not been tampered with in travel and the sender of the word is honest to goodness individual, who is likewise known to the collector. Indeed, even the sender of the world can't change the message once it has been sent. It can't be started by someone else, are transportable, and can likewise be time-stamped naturally.

It depends on the idea of open key cryptography. People in crucial general cryptography requires two keys, one that is open and known to every concerned gathering and the other one that is a mystery and is known just to the sender. Both keys are connected scientifically. One key is utilized to scramble the message while alternate decodes the encoded signal. Distinctive approaches are being used for this reason.

Advantages of Electronic Signing

Confirmation: now and again it is hard to recognize whether the message got is from a genuine source or not. Be that as it may, with the utilization of Electronic Signing the source can be verified. This will guarantee the collector that the message was sent from the planned sender. They are profoundly utilized in money related setting as a result of their consistent quality.

Respectability: It keeps the modification of message. A common word is for the most part in the threat of being adjusted before achieving its coveted goal. To guarantee this does not occur, Signing ends up essential. The encoded figure won't be effectively comprehended and accordingly won't be tempered.

Utilization of Electronic Signing in the Business World

The headway in innovation everywhere throughout the world has brought about the end of abundance paperwork and has decreased the utilization of conventional marks too. The majority of the contacts and records are sent over the web instead of through the post. Consequently, the association picking to go advanced likewise needs security for their reports.

The contact executed online ought to be as ironclad as the agreement marked within sight of both the gatherings. So they choose electronic adaptation of conventional marks by utilizing the Electronic Signing system. There is a lot of credible programming accessible in the market that is being used by associations to create open and private keys and subsequently scrambles their message.

It is broadly utilized in online money related exchanges, internet business organizations, banks, clinics, incomplete web-based business organizations and nearly by every one of the associations leading their business on the web.

Encryption is an incredibly important tool for keeping your data safe. When your files are encrypted, they are completely unreadable without the correct encryption key. If someone steals your encrypted files, they won't be able to do anything with them.

There are two types of encryption: hardware and software. Both offer different advantages. So, what are these methods and why do they matter?

Software Encryption

As the name implies, software encryption uses software tools to encrypt your data. Some examples of these tools include the BitLocker drive encryption feature of Microsoft Windows and the 1Password password manager. Both use encryption tools to protect information on your PC, smartphone, or tablet.

Software encryption typically relies on a password; give the right password, and your files will be decrypted, otherwise they remain locked. With encryption enabled, it is passed through a special algorithm that scrambles your data as it is written to disk. The same software then unscrambles data as it is read from the disk for an authenticated user.

Pros

Software encryption is typically quite cheap to implement, making it very popular with developers. In addition, software-based encryption routines do not require any additional hardware.

Cons

Software encryption is only as secure as the rest of your computer or smartphone. If a hacker can crack your password, the encryption is immediately undone.

Software encryption tools also share the processing resources of your computer, which can cause the entire machine to slow down as data is encrypted/decrypted. You will also find that opening and closing encrypted files is much slower than normal because the process is relatively resource intensive, particularly for higher levels of encryption.

Hardware encryption

At the heart of hardware encryption is a separate processor dedicated to the task of authentication and encryption. Hardware encryption is increasingly common on mobile devices. The TouchID fingerprint scanner on Apple iPhones is a good example.

The technology still relies on a special key to encrypt and decrypt data, but this is randomly generated by the encryption processor. Often times, hardware encryption devices replace traditional passwords with biometric logons (like fingerprints) or a PIN number that is entered on an attached keypad.

Pros

Hardware encryption is safer than software encryption because the encryption process is separate from the rest of the machine. This makes it much harder to intercept or break.

The use of a dedicated processor also relieves the burden on the rest of your device, making the encryption and decryption process much faster.

Cons

Typically, hardware-based encrypted storage is much more expensive than a software tool. For instance, BitLocker is included for free with all new versions of Microsoft Windows, but an encrypted USB thumb drive is quite expensive, especially when compared to an unencrypted alternative.

If the hardware decryption processor fails, it becomes extremely hard to access your information.

The Data Recovery Challenge

Encrypted data is a challenge to recover. Even by recovering the raw sectors from a failed drive, it is still encrypted, which means it is still unreadable. Some software encryption systems, like BitLocker, have built-in recovery mechanisms, but you must set up your recovery options in advance.

Hardware encrypted devices don't typically have these additional recovery options. Many have a design to prevent decryption in the event of a component failure, stopping hackers from disassembling them.

The fastest and most effective way to deal with data loss on an encrypted device is to ensure you have a complete backup stored somewhere safe. For your PC, this may mean copying data to another encrypted device. For other devices, like your smartphone, backing up to the Cloud provides a quick and simple economy copy that you can restore from. As an added bonus, most Cloud services now encrypt their users' data too. Apple® utilizes Cloud storage, but if you don't set it up before a failure of your device, you can take advantage of Apple recovery offered by many data recovery businesses.

What to do if You Have a Problem

COMMON TECHNIQUES USED BY ENTERPRISES TO SECURE DATA

In the present computerized age, data is power, and all necessary info is at present put away on ensured servers worked by organizations themselves or by outsider administrators. If an organization can't shield its information from access by unapproved people, the outcome can be destroyed for the organization itself and also all merchants and partners required with the organization. Such necessary information which is generally ensured utilizing driving data security administrations can be used by unapproved people to perpetrate violations, for example, insider exchanging, delicate settling and so forth. Nations everywhere throughout the world have laws to anticipate such unapproved information get to and resistance with the rules is the cognizable offense with the organizations paying mighty fines to the administration, if the information safety efforts are ruptured. Notwithstanding, a joint inquiry that emerges is the means by which to organizations guarantee that their information remains shielded from access by unapproved people. A portion of the security arrangements intended to ensure appropriate information insurance are:

Open Authentication Mechanisms

Open validation instruments are generally connected to restrain the availability of online endeavor arrangements, particularly in cases, where the regularly utilized User ID and Password-based confirmation systems are considered to be deficient. Ordinarily employed open verification systems incorporate Open ID, Security Assertion Markup Language (SAML) and X.509 Certificate.

Open ID

OpenID is a leading open standard, which notices methodology by which, venture clients might be confirmed utilizing a decentralized framework. The fundamental advantages of OpenID are the end of the need for administrations to give their very own structures and besides, the power gave to clients to uniting their very own advanced characters. Clients are permitted to make their very own OpenID record and utilize a similar record data to sign on to any site or online arrangement, which acknowledges OpenID validation.

SAML (Security Assertion Markup Language)

SAML, a protected innovation the OASIS Security Services Technical Committee, is an open standard because of the XML stage. SAML underpins the trading of information required for approval and validation between two separate security areas, for example, between a specialist co-op and a personality supplier. The current SAML details either suggest or command the utilization of TLS 1.0 or SSL 3.0 for giving transport-level security, while, XML Encryption and XML Signature are required to provide message-level security.

X.509 Certificate

X.509 Certificate is an ITU-T (International Telecom Union-Telecommunication) standard for Privilege Management Infrastructure (PMI) and basic open foundation (PKI). Enter determinations incorporated into the X.509 Certificate combine standard organizations as for affirmation way approval calculation, property authentications, declaration renouncement records, and open vital endorsements. Adaptation 3.0 of the X.509 is exceptionally flexible and fit for supporting lattices and scaffolds separated from the strict progressive system based arrangement of authentication specialists bolstered by the X.500 standard, which was for the most part utilized by nations to satisfy settlement prerequisites identified with state character data sharing. In the X.509 framework, an accreditation specialist is permitted to issue an endorsement restricting key to an elective name, (for example, a DNS passage/email address) or to a particular recognized name (like the X.500 framework). By utilizing the X.509 affirmation, an organization can convey it's confided in root endorsement to its representatives to empower endeavor broad access to the organization's PKI framework using any internet browser.

COMPUTERIZED SIGNATURE

This is a standout amongst the most widely recognized procedures to guarantee the legitimacy of advanced reports. A computerized mark is contained a numerical plan, and a substantially superior mark, as a result, infers that the transmitted message was gotten in its unique shape and was not adjusted amid the travel time frame. The utilization of computerized mark is most regular if there should be an occurrence of money related exchanges and programming dissemination, as the two cases require better security than identify altering or falsification. Computerized mark is regularly utilized reciprocally with the electronic score, be that as it may, an electronic score is a substantially broader term, which is being used about any information, with the choice of conveying a mark. By and large, the science plans of Digital

Signatures are cryptography based, which on amend execution, are more hard to produce when contrasted with transcribed marks. Aside from budgetary exchanges and programming dissemination, Digital Signatures are additionally found in messages, contacts, and messages transmitted utilizing a cryptographic convention. Prevalent security can likewise be given by sparing the private key produced for use on a key card.

Encryption

Security of information whether putting away on a server or transmitted to others is dependably a noteworthy worry for undertakings everywhere throughout the world. One of the customarily utilized systems to guarantee absolute security is the utilization of SSL (Secure Socket Layer), which keeps the unapproved access of information to some degree. Notwithstanding, SSL is unequipped for anchoring the info if numerous mediators are included amid exchange. Encryption is firmly identified with cryptography, and it guarantees that the information is rendered mixed up except if the client has the right key to unscramble the message. Encryption is one of the primary methods to guarantee proceeded with insurance of delicate data for information put away on portability gadgets and servers.

Character Provisioning

Character provisioning alludes to making, keeping up and de-enacting different proof qualities and items, which exist in numerous applications, registries or frameworks in the event of different intuitive or robotized business capacities. The procedure of personality arrangement regularly incorporates the accompanying methods centralized change control, assigned client organization, united client organization, self-administration work process and also change engendering. Client objects are ordinarily used to recognize different beneficiaries, for example, accomplices, merchants, clients, workers and so forth. Enter administrations incorporated into personality provisioning include access to big business registering assets, approved access to ensured database things, consideration inside a confined client index, access to scrambled endeavor email and so on.

These are just a couple of the regular strategies utilized by undertakings to guarantee information security, as new advancements and dangers develop, endeavors are relied upon to acquaint new safety efforts planned with ensuring corporate information as per the continually evolving conditions.

Associations using cryptography for anchoring private data have the decision of equipment and programming constructed arrangements depending in light of the idea of the information needing encryption. The weakest connection in the chain is the cryptographic keys used to scramble and decode the information. This is because of the continually expanding handling intensity of the modern PCs and the period it might take to trade off the keys through a thorough critical inquiry. Subsequently, these associations should frequently renounce, refresh and circulate the keys to the pertinent gatherings with a specific end goal to diminish the danger of interior and outer dangers.

Numerous parts, including saving money and administrative, have sufficient energy devouring undertaking of following and overseeing consistently expanding quantities of keys to guarantee the privilege keys are in the correct place at the ideal time. The broad measures of keys required for the everyday tasks of utilizations utilizing crypto will prompt a multitude of executives if the keys are overseen physically. Consequently, necessary mechanized administration frameworks are presently a need for these associations on the off chance that they are to keep over the outstanding task at hand and decrease their administrator costs.

Enter administration will come in numerous varieties with some more reasonable for big business settings while others are more adaptable, intended for the enormous quantities of keys as used in the keeping money industry. Diverse necessities require unique arrangements. Nonetheless, there are some broad issues which must be tended to if the usage of such frameworks is to be useful regarding usefulness, consistency, accessibility and keeping costs at the very least. A short rundown of best practice methodology is underneath:

- De-bring together encryption and decoding
- Centralized lifecycle key administration
- Automated key circulation and refreshing
- Future confirmation - supporting different gauges, e.g., PCI DSS, Sarbanes-Oxley, and FIPS 140-2
- Support for all real equipment and programming security modules to maintain a strategic distance from merchant tie-in
- Flexible key ascribes to dispose of the printed material.
- Comprehensive accessible alter apparent review logs
- Transparent and streamlined procedures

- Based on open guidelines to Minimize advancement time when coordinating new applications

With a framework joining these components, the critical administration can wipe out a significant number of the dangers related to human blunder and purposeful assaults on the secret information. It might likewise permit the adaptability for giving security to applications which may be some way or another have been considered too expensive for cryptography.

Notwithstanding industry or arrangement an association may pick, the above rundown, at any rate, ought to be the foundation of any essential administration framework, to empower an abnormal state of security as well as to enhance forms and give short and long-haul funds.

EARNING A CYBERSECURITY CERTIFICATE

Cybersecurity preparing with the final product in gaining an authentication gives you a few ways to consider. A few colleges and schools have cybersecurity programs, and additionally, other industry affiliations and establishments, have classes which come full circle in a cybersecurity declaration.

Thought should be given to the essential focal point of the cybersecurity testament program. A few projects cook more towards the "administrative" side of cybersecurity, though some different projects, similar to the testament track at Stanford University, have a point of convergence on the specialized team of cybersecurity and need you to have a base learning in programming or advancement.

Likewise, the ways or techniques for gaining an endorsement shift. You can win one either on the web or face to face. A few schools and learning roads offer either; however, programs exist which you let settle on the decision of on the internet or classroom-based preparing.

A degree in cybersecurity can be the ultimate objective, through utilizing specific testament courses if that is the thing that you want. A degree in cybersecurity will assuredly necessitate that extra courses be taken. Furthermore, thought should be given concerning the assets required for those additional courses and the subsequent degree.

Offer idea to what you need to escape your preparation too, notwithstanding merely the testament. You most likely need an intensive comprehension of them, for the most part, acknowledged standard procedures related to the field of cybersecurity. Think along the lines of "what does the business, all in all, observe as the prerequisites for an intensive comprehension of cybersecurity"? Too, what would you like to escape your cybersecurity preparing, notwithstanding the declaration you will acquire?

Additionally, what style of learning suits you best? Improve face to face with direction from an educator? Somebody, you can make inquiries and get tweaked reactions from? Or then again would you say you are to a greater degree a self-starter who can search out the appropriate responses you require on the web? Would you be able to inspire yourself, or do you need some outside push to motivate you to learn?

While getting the testament is an objective all by itself, don't make that the main focal point of your training here. There is a whole other world to be increased through preparing to win your cybersecurity testament. The factual finding out about the subject of cybersecurity ought to be the main push behind gaining your authentication. Since without that topic learning, having the declaration itself won't mean everything that much. Ensure you consider how you will best take in more about cybersecurity all in all.

CYBERSECURITY: PLAYING DEFENSE AND OFFENSE IN CYBERSPACE AND THE ECONOMY

In the long early stretches of cyber-attacks, associations would hold up to be assaulted before they built up an extensive arrangement and reaction to the assailant. The assault would render the associations' system nearness pointless and down for a considerable length of time. A few reasons cyberattack could severely disable a system at the beginning of this vindictive conduct are insufficient focused research on safeguarding and counteracting and the absence of an organized exertion between private industry and the administration.

Since the principal understood and across the board cyberattack in the mid-1990's, numerous experts out in the open and private associations have industriously been considering and taking a shot at the issue of cyber-attacks. At first security organizations like Norton, McAfee, Trend Micro, and so forth moved toward the problem from a responsive stance. They knew programmers/malignant aggressors would strike. The objective of what is presently called Intrusion Detection Systems (IDS) was to recognize a fatal assailant before an enemy of infection, Trojan steed, or worm was utilized to strike. On the off chance that the assailant could hit the system, security experts would analyze the code. Once the lawwas explained, a reaction or "fix" was connected to the contaminated machine(s). The "fix" is currently called a mark, and they are reliably downloaded over the system as week by week updates to shield against known assaults. Even though IDS is a sit back and watch pose, security experts have become significantly more advanced in their methodology, and it keeps on developing as a significant aspect of the arms stockpile.

Security experts started taking a gander at the issue from a preventive edge. This moved the cybersecurity business from cautious to hostile mode. They were currently investigating how to keep an assault on a framework or system. Given this line of reasoning, an Intrusion Prevention Systems (IPS) called Snort (2010) was before long presented. Grunt is a blend IDS and IPS open source programming accessible for FREE download. Utilizing IDS/IPS programming like Snort enables security experts to be proactive in the cybersecurity field. Even though IPS enables security experts to play offense and added protection, they don't lay on their shrubs nor do they quit observing crafted by noxious assailants which fills inventiveness, creative ability, and development. It likewise permits security experts that protect the cyber world to remain equivalent or one stage in front of assailants.

Cybersecurity additionally plays a hostile and guarded job in the economy. In its cybersecurity business, The University of Maryland University College (2012) states there will be "fifty-thousand occupations accessible in cybersecurity throughout the following ten years." The school has been running this business for over two years. At the point when the company initially started running, they cited thirty-thousand employments. They have balanced the gauge higher in light of concentrates and also the legislature and private industry distinguishing cybersecurity as a basic need to safeguard basic foundation.

Cybersecurity can play financial resistance by ensuring these employments which manage national security concerns and should remain the in the United States. The cybersecurity business is driven by national security in the administration domain and protected innovation (IP) in the private business space. Numerous U.S. organizations whined to the administration about outside nations howdy jacking their product thoughts and developments through state-supported and sorted out wrongdoing programmers. Given that foreign countries excuse state-supported national security and licensed innovation assaults, it would be to the advantage of organizations to discover human capital inside the shores of the United States to play out the obligations and errands required.

Incomplete attack mode side, Cybersecurity can goad improvement and increment the ranges of abilities of occupants in areas like Prince George's County, Maryland which sits in the epicenter of Cybersecurity for the province of Maryland and the country. Sovereign George's Community College is the home of Cyber watch and the focal center point for cybersecurity preparing and best practices that get pushed out to other junior colleges that are a piece of the consortium. The objective of these junior colleges is to adjust the training offered to understudies with aptitudes that organizations say should have been "workforce prepared." It is likewise a rich enrolling ground for tech organizations the nation over to distinguish and employ human cash-flow to put on the cutting edges of the U.S. battle in cybersecurity.

CHAPTER FIVE

5 REASONS YOU NEED A CYBERSECURITY PLAN

We have all lived in the publicity around cybersecurity and how if we don't focus, it can turn into our lousy dream, one where even the best corporate securities and government won't have the capacity to intercede. There is no prerequisite of any evidence or insights to demonstrate the risk: Cyberattacks is our world. Why has this change from a chance to reality occurred?

The capacity of a few associations to manage splitting and hacking has decreased altogether.

Individuals taking a shot at cyber-attacks are more educated when contrasted with a normal IT proficient. Gone are where novice programmers were assaulting our frameworks. Today, these cyber-attacksare made by fear-based oppressors and wrongdoing syndicates.

Individuals safeguarding against the cyberattack are utilizing the wrong barrier instrument. The dangers are more muddled. It is much the same as a war, with a few aggressors, a vast number of targets, and no real objective.

So what would we be able to do to ensure our association? Indeed, our countries and presidents are going outlaws to help battle this, however, is it remarkably going to stop? No, we have to reevaluate our IT methodology all alone and put in place a framework and process that will help our security.

Here are the best five reasons concerning why you require a Cybersecurity plan:

- There are high shots that you have recognized the wrong danger, which makes your methodology off-base. You may have a considerable measure of security systems set up, yet what the number of them is as yet substantial according to the present market situation? You will never know the appropriate response if you don't require the cognizant exertion to discover. In this way, you have to remain up and to come and make an arrangement that battles most new dangers.

- Making a committed procedure for cybersecurity and refreshing it consistently is an exertion in itself, which is generally not generally present. Keeping that procedure new and making it particular will enable you to impact security choices to the most.

- The single word to crush responsive protection. We don't have to actualize anything extravagant when we know it will fall flat. Be that as it may, how does an association turn out to be proactive? It starts with making a cybersecurity technique, which considers the uniqueness of your association and plans an establishment because of that.

- The procedure is the center for any association. It helps in settling on a brought together choice, and a beyond any doubt approach to comprehend and resolve an issue. In any case, this isn't merely irregular standards, however particular objectives, choices, and targets to confront the difficulties.

- A definitive execution metric for associations is execution. Utilize it to feature how you perform in challenges, the methodology you would use for accomplishing positive outcomes. Just a technique will enable you to distinguish your association's security position. Keep in mind that you have to set a metric in light of the dangers that you have looked previously, and to those, you haven't encountered yet. Making a security plan for yesterday's technique won't insure against the risks of tomorrow.

Cybersecurity

The more significant part of you believe that the best way to deal with protecting is at the system or code-level, and unquestionably that is one lump of a riddle. What's more, that is the thing we have to skip, as of not long ago we have been moving the riddle pieces around with no beyond any doubt arrangement. Cybersecurity is a greater picture that demonstrates to us that it is urgent to comprehend that riddle; as opposed to discovering two-three huge pieces and depending on those to finish the photo.

10 CYBERSECURITY MYTHS THAT EVERY ORGANIZATION SHOULD KNOW

Legend #1:"Digital hazard" has a place with a select class

Grouping association chance as merely "digital hazard" will undermine the gravity of the danger. William H. Saito, Special Advisor of the Cabinet Office for the Government of Japan expresses, "There's no such thing as "digital hazard" - it's the hazard." in his much-saw piece in Forbes magazine. He instructs peruses that digital hazard includes protected innovation to the wellbeing of faculty and that it needs rise to consideration from senior administration and official group.

Legend #2: Cybersecurity is another type of danger we haven't experienced

It was perhaps familiar to lean toward trusting cybersecurity as a test not at all like you've looked previously. However, history will disclose to you nothing's new. Back in the Victorian period, when correspondences and trade experienced a change with advancements in innovation, the danger saw was the same. Wrestling among horse riding, broadcast, and remote radio was similarly - if not more- - a vanguard encounter

Fantasy #3: Knocking down cybersecurity to an "IT issue."

Digital dangers when assigned as "IT chance" will empower overrunning through the whole framework. It's essential to know, digital threats cut crosswise over offices, and that is what is threatening. Data once digitized, there's no reserving digital danger to an office.

Fantasy #4: Cyber-attacks are standard - a few associations are assaulted ordinary

Checking the number of cyber-attacks is a vain exercise since it is equal to tallying microscopic organisms. What makes a difference is an effect. Some of the time numbers lie. The assaults that are frustrated by elemental resistances are additionally considered now and again. Along these lines, they can be a conflating blend. Savvy activity measures the dangers and organizes the best approach to an arrangement to with them.

Legend #5: Relying on programming is sufficiently protected

Albeit great programming is critical to guard cyberattacks. It isn't sufficient to see programming in confinement. Individuals are the numero uno danger. It is you put resources into preparing your assets and enhance the ease of use of digital programming, in this manner, striking an excellent harmony among well-being and comfort of use.

Legend #6: Hackers do no objective SMEs

The presumption that programmers do no lean toward SMEs is a problematic one. SMEs not putting fittingly in cybersecurity is the thing that supports assailants. Programmers can work without much stretch access to your data, which could be significant. A report distributed in 2015 by HM Government affirms the helplessness with 74% of SMEs revealing a security rupture.

Fantasy #7: Manufacturers are in charge of a safe framework

Genuine. Gadget creators ought to be more dependable in making secure items that are powerful. Be that as it may, usually individuals who are flighty and problematic. Individuals discover approaches to sidestep security by utilizing gadgets that are not all that anchored - cell phones and tablets.

Legend #8: My data does not merit taking

No individual needs their private data to be stolen. Putting away and sharing data on the web is continually going to be an issue, for fear that we manage it sooner. End-to-end encryption through a VPN is a safe method for sharing data over the web.

Legend #9: Internet of things abridges powerlessness

The coming of IP V6 will usher another period of the network. All gadgets like TVs, clothes washers, iceboxes, dishwashers et cetera will before long be allowed an IP. You will have remote access to your home gadgets. Be that as it may, by outline, it makes your home more defenseless than any other time in recent memory. It is trusted that producers will before long perceive gadgets are potential courses to our delicate data and act so.

Legend #10: 'Programmers' are the most significant risk

There will be awful people doing offensive things. In any case, disregarding the organizations that occasionally put on a show to be our controller is additionally unsafe. Governments have been surrounding strategies to have the unique power over your information. Any such endeavor must be contradicted at a strategic level with the goal that the trust among the web clients is maintained.

Cybersecurity counseling is a developing sub-field inside business administrations, made merely more essential as the page of digital fighting increments as of late and months. Since none, however, the exceptionally most prominent organizations have the necessary aptitudes in-house, data security counseling is a need for most SME's, who might commit this kind of consultancy benefit out of the blue.

Numerous entrepreneurs locate that connecting with the administrations of a cybersecurity advisor can convey positive incentive regarding legitimate and administrative consistency, shirking of information security breaks, and streamlining of their business forms. A developing number of organizations are looking to accomplish compatibility with ISO 27001, the global standard for an Information Security Management System (ISMS). This is a prime territory where the abilities of a data security expert can yield profits for a business that uses its advisors shrewdly.

A counseling commitment can be separated into stages. The term of each step can differ broadly, contingent upon such factors as the measure of the organization, the phase of preliminary work that has been done, the staff time accessible, the level of current ability at the organization - and, apparently, the need given to it at the administration level.

As a rule, in any case, the periods of cybersecurity counseling will take the accompanying general shape:

Inception: Determine the extent of the task (the entire association or only a subset?) and assign spending plan and staff. Select a data security advisor and a lead contact individual.

Arranging: Plan the Information Security Management System that will frame the yield of the task. Play out a hazard investigation and construct every important choice concerning its return.

Usage: Implement the ISMS for a reasonable period, and address any slight underlying issues.

Checking: Regularly screen and survey the task of the ISMS, and banner up any territories which are offering ascend to issues or sub-standard execution.

Change: Take particular and quantifiable strides to enhance the activity of the ISMS.

The cycle of checking and change is a nonstop one, and may even include assisting cybersecurity counseling input (particularly if the association wants to accomplish confirmation to the ISO 27001 standard). The data security expert can give essential contribution at each period of the procedure, and will a while later be accessible to help if any issues are experienced then on.

Cybersecurity counseling is a vital business benefit that can have a genuine effect on the information security of an association. With the expanding event of digital assaults and information breaks, an ever-increasing number of organizations are finding that making utilization of data security counseling administrations is a real interest later on of the business.

BIGGEST THREAT TO ENTERPRISE CYBERSECURITY - THIRD-PARTY REMOTE SUPPORT

This attestation addresses all areas, not merely fund. Headways in arrange security items have made it troublesome for unapproved people to get too big business frameworks specifically. The new route in is through advantaged accomplices. Undertaking innovation sellers (retail, healing facilities, clubhouse, banks, vitality suppliers, government offices) are regularly given system accreditations to bolster their clients remotely.

Remote help is significant as innovation enhances, however the most usually utilized techniques for the association - VPNs and work area sharing instruments - are not anchor for outsider access. It is this defenseless merchant association that is by and large exceedingly abused by programmers. Giving over the keys to the kingdom to each innovation accomplice is never again a choice in this post-"Year of the Breach" world.

Two of the most significant information ruptures on record, Target, and Home Depot, were both caused by the blunder of outsider merchant arrange certifications. This isn't a fortuitous event; this is a pattern. VPNs will lead others down this same risky street whenever utilized for remote help since programmers are concentrating on outsider merchants to access their more lucrative targets.

Anchoring your system from unapproved get to is necessary, yet it's similarly vital to have a far-reaching review of approved access also. How you deal with the "keys to the kingdom" straightforwardly mirrors the general security of your system.

Outsider sellers need to get to their client's systems for an assortment of reasons. However, the strategy forgets to should be observed and secure. Remote help programming and arrangements are utilized to increase quick access and resolve issues - VPNs and work area sharing devices are generally ordinary. Nonetheless, if we take a gander at the Home Depot and Target, it turns out to be evident that the most popular arrangements are presently turning into the issue.

A VPN elective is essential to anchor any responsibility in remote access. Outsider sellers frequently share their VPN qualifications; this restrains the capacity to track changes and spot inconsistencies. Numerous organizations depend on a VPN to give remote access to representatives, yet a VPN option ought to be utilized when working with outsider merchants. Work area sharing devices are useful for the coordinated effort, yet amid seller arrange to bolster they make apparitions that leave no follow. If we take in anything from Home Depot and Target, it ought to be to give careful consideration to both who you offer accreditations to and how you oversee and screen that seller's entrance.

The infographic beneath outlines the dangers all innovation suppliers and undertaking system security experts should know about as they address strategies for secure remote help associations.

Quantum Internet and Cybersecurity

Quantum processing can change the manner in which that we utilize PCs and the web. Not at all like customary twofold figuring, in which bits must appear as either a 0 or a 1, in quantum processing it is feasible for Q-bits, as they are called, to take the middle of the road frames. A Q-bit can be both 0 and 1 in the meantime. This expands the scope of potential outcomes and empowers quantum processing to be much more intense than regular registering.

The speed at which a PC can work is generally subject to its transistors. A quantum transistor can expand the speed of a PC since it can work fundamentally quicker than a regular conductor. Quantum transistors have been made utilizing the ideas of quantum material science that empower particles to impart crosswise over space without really contacting. In the quantum transistor, one light emission is used to control the properties of another light emission. This implies data can be imparted much more quickly than with a regular conductor. Data can be exchanged without the requirement for any substance to venture to every part of the separation. The improvement of quantum figuring will rely on the disclosure of techniques for outfitting the intensity of quantum trap or of creating superconductors.

The improvement of quantum figuring and the quantum web has some significant ramifications for cybersecurity. Instead of just responding to dangers and issues once they have just emerged, the quantum web may empower us to adopt a considerably more proactive strategy to cybersecurity.

This is on account of the quantum web will empower us to handle security at the level of bits, which isn't a methodology that is conceivable with regular figuring. As of now, somewhat should either resister a 0 or a 1, yet in quantum figuring, it is workable for bits to enlist both 0 and one all the while. At the point when a quantum bit accepts its esteem, it is unimaginable for the bit to be replicated without the sender getting to be mindful of it. This is because replicating the bit would make its state change. Any danger to security would in this manner be identified instantly, at the bit level. Web clients would dependably know when their safety or protection had been debilitated, which would make secret assaults outlandish.

DATA SCIENCE AND ITS RISING IMPORTANCE IN CYBERSECURITY [BIG DATA ANALYTICS]

Information Science and Cybersecurity - what is enormous information investigation? For what reason realizes machine applications so vital? For what reason did InfoSec Professionals require to find out about DS? What to think about "information bots" as an information science proficient? Contrasts in information science versus machine learning? How to split cybersecurity occupations with information science advantage?

DS is a multi-sided field that utilizations logical systems, strategies, calculations, and security practices to extricate data and bits of knowledge.

With the assistance of DS devices, for example, Machine Learning and Big Data Analytics, organizations would now be able to gain admittance to significant bits of knowledge covered up inside gigantic informational indexes.

This is the place DS can help make a critical and enduring effect.

DS and cybersecurity, two of the most mainstream vocation ways, are on an impact course. Extremely intelligent, prepared, senior directors don't wholly comprehend the significance, or the complexities, of DS and cybersecurity. "There's a troubling surge in the digital security arrangements space to utilize the terms machine learning, examination, and DS related to security items. The CERT Data Science and Cybersecurity Symposium featured advances in DS, looked into government utilize cases, and exhibited related devices. Connected DS for Cyber Security. In this day and age, we are ambushed by consistently expanding measures of information and progressively advanced assaults. The program is intended to assemble understudies' learning and build up their mastery in arrange security, cryptography, DS, and enormous information examination. The NACE Center and BHEF directed inquiry into two abilities liable to be essential later on the economy: information investigation and cybersecurity aptitudes. An information researcher is an expert with a mix of skills in software engineering, arithmetic and cybersecurity space mastery. Digital

Security is a quickly developing field in an ever-interconnected world. Realize why it makes a difference and what information science needs to do with it. Information science, alongside innovations, for example, machine learning and human-made consciousness, has discovered its way into many security items. Driving specialists in the fields of information science and cybersecurity examining the scope of subjects identified with the job - DS has in tending to the issues.

The segment of learning will outline the between the connection between a few information administration, investigation and choice help systems and techniques generally embraced in. With computerization and AI ready to get occupations that people require them to, information examination and cybersecurity may think that it's less demanding to procure talented representatives. Although machine learning instruments are usually utilized in various applications, the enormous blast of cutting-edge examination in cybersecurity is yet to come. What's more, that will intrigue see the future apparatuses to cop up with. Fingers crossed.

Cybersecurity and the U.S. Substance Industry: Expect the Unexpected

Cyberterrorism, Cyberespionage, Cyber assault.
Regardless of how you portray the ongoing attacks against Sony Pictures, the administration was not prepared. No objective is each prepared, yet the industry is faultless with practical, proactive, close collaboration with the U.S. Government.

Most likely digital assaults against the United States will turn out to be more predominant. People, gatherings or nations that don't have the way to assault us physically will swing to the Internet as an option. Assaults are anything but trying to deny and to pinpoint mindful gatherings is to a significant degree troublesome. Was North Korea retaliating for Sony's booked arrival of a political parody film or would it say it was an inside activity? Sony is an ongoing best-known target, however throughout the most recent quite a long while there have been others.

In 2012, more than 30,000 Saudi Aramco PCs were obliterated by a wiper infection. Other late casualties have included substance firms, Anthem, eBay, the Montana Health Department, and even Domino's Pizza:

Song of praise: Hackers accessed the private information of 80 million previous and current individuals from the country's second-biggest wellbeing guarantor. The break uncovered Social Security numbers, wage information, birthday events, and road and email addresses. Specialists speculate Chinese programmers (2015).

Domino's Pizza: Hacking bunch Rex Mundi held the pizza tie to recover more than 600,000 Belgian and French custom records. Mundi requested $40,000 from the chain (2014).

P.F. Chang's: Thousands of stolen credit and charge cards utilized at the eatery network went available to be purchased online (2014).

Montana Health Department: Data break bargained up to 1.3 million safeguarded with touchy data sold on the bootleg market (2014).

eBay: Hackers stole individual records of 233 million clients.

Saudi Aramco: Computer infection deleted information on seventy-five percent of Aramco's corporate PC's - archives, messages, spreadsheets - supplanting every last bit of it with a picture of a consuming American banner (2012).

Compound firms in the USA, UK, and Bangladesh: Nitro infection focused on principally privately owned businesses associated with research, improvement, and assembling of synthetic compounds and propelled materials. The objective of the assaults had all the earmarks of being to gather licensed innovation, plan and collecting forms (2012).

Our present way to deal with digital barrier is outdated against refined, industrious interruptions. Luckily, no digital assault on synthetic offices so far has brought about arrivals of harmful synthetics. In light of late disruption and considering the kinds of synthetic compounds produced and put away at substance plants, similar to chlorine, it is essential that the Government and industry work firmly together and put resources into the foundation because of cybersecurity.

The American Chemistry Council (ACC), our country's most established exchange affiliation, speaks to organizations occupied with the matter of science. It perceives the invitation to battle! For instance, all ACC part organizations, as a feature of their responsibility under the Responsible Care Security Code, evaluate cybersecurity vulnerabilities, execute subtle security elements, and prepare representatives. Capable Care organizations are pioneers in false security and work intimately with the government, state, and nearby knowledge offices to protect networks. Best practices to get ready and react to interruptions, and drive data sharing between individuals, are additionally tried through part organization support in the Department of Homeland Security's Cyber Storm practice arrangement. Each Cyber Storm exertion, directed biennially, expands on exercises gained from earlier genuine interruptions, ensuring that members perceive, and make a corrective move, to most new dangers.

Dissimilar to numerous other primary foundation divisions, the government manages cybersecurity for synthetic concoctions. Under the CFATS (Chemical Facility Anti-Terrorism Standards) program, the legislature distinguishes and directs high-chance concoction offices to guarantee that they have security set up to decrease dangers related with these synthetic compounds. In 2014, the President marked enactment that gave a premise to the continuation and refinement of the program to address the assurance of business systems and process control frameworks.

Forceful advances must proceed with the goal that we can safeguard ourselves from digital assault. Enterprises must comprehend the helplessness of their systems. Substance industry members and governments must work firmly together, aware of fundamental scholarly insurance prerequisites. Cybersecurity, or absence of it, impacts all of us. A hacking interruption knows no outskirts. Global collaboration ought to be reinforced to give the general population affirmation that everything that should be possible is being finished.

The assaults against Sony, Aramco, and others feature our vulnerabilities. We have to go to the outrageous to secure ourselves and keep an unimaginable fiasco from happening.

Mechanical advances advantage our general public, yet there is a dark side, and it focuses on digital security. I am keen on got notification from peruses about digital security and steps taken by the substance business to ensure the general population.

CYBERSECURITY - LIAR, LIAR

The upheaval is here. Each fruitful, real unrest in history had two essential sides to it, the individuals who profited and the already enabled. The Internet was not made for the majority, or by a consortium of the overall population with your best advantages considered. The beforehand allowed global community is from numerous points of view now casualties of PC frameworks, especially in respect to the web.

Its utilization has continuously supported the most exceedingly resourced and gifted. Also, appropriate programming and equipment advancement are continually extending, much quicker than we can take in advantage from the earlier emphasis. It resembles opening interminably settled dolls. Also, organizations are always endeavoring to outflank every others' items concerning functional attributes (estimate, speed, limit, portability, brightness, the simplicity of use, interface, network, security, and so on.), and beat their rivals to deals. The recipients are generally the best-advertised items; the washouts are those of us living with and every so often consumed by, neglected useful guarantees.

Below average execution of PC framework segments happens consistently for some reasons. Also, information spills, hacked information, and other data misfortunes occur intentionally, wrongly and are spilled into people in general field by open organizations, private organizations, and programmers every day as grievous components of the insurgency in our data access and utilize.

The natural hazard has never been clarified to general society. The more significant part of the overall population does not comprehend what they can and can't anticipate from individual and business frameworks, and have a couple of sensible alternatives concerning the execution of a related business. Who might have expected a budgetary enterprise that gains considerably more than a billion dollars in every year, with around 9,000 workers in fourteen nations, and exchanged on the NYSE to not take choice consideration of information endowed to it? What's more, what new college alumni who is always besieged by corporate mental board applications would trust that an organization to which they are applying has top administration that gave themselves a four-month window through which to parachute before letting the rest of the world would think about their corporate information break issues - envision the volumes of stock and alternatives these corporate pioneers sold to maintain a strategic distance from their cheapening. A great many people will have the capacity to add to their tributes -

Basic Cybersecurity Steps for You to Take

One of the most significant difficulties we are looked with on the Internet is digital assaults.

Dangers to our economy, national security, online networks, and families rely upon how successful we are at shielding ourselves from digital assaults from Internet predators. Here are a couple of steps that will enhance your online security.

To start with, ensure you have against infection programming and firewalls designed legitimately. Ensure they are refreshed routinely, too. Ordinary new dangers are found, so staying up with the latest and current makes it less demanding to ensure you and your family, or business from assaults. Most enemies of infection and firewall programs have programmed refreshes accessible for you to arrange.

Another security safety measure method is to refresh your working framework and indispensable program programming. These product refreshes give the most recent assurance against vindictive assaults. Once more, a large portion of these basic programming programs has programmed refreshes accessible for you to turn on.

Make sure to back up your vital documents. Duplicate them onto removable circles you can store in a sheltered place, best at another area other than where your PC is at.

Know Who You're Dealing With

In all undertakings, it's likewise vital for you to comprehend what you're getting into, and who you're managing particularly on the Internet. You can't pass judgment on somebody's character or thought processes by basically taking a gander at a profile picture, MLM blog, or site. Numerous tricksters online imitate authentic MLM, offshoot, and locally situated organizations when they have ulterior thought processes. Ensure you do some examination before making any buys of items or administrations from people or organizations on the Internet.

At long last, ensure your passwords-keep them in a safe place. Best practices propose utilizing longer passwords which incorporate letters and images. Every ninety days change your secret word and abstain from using essential words. Utilize unique passwords for every one of your online records.

The Next Cyber Victim Could Be You

The news about Equifax's information break and the long queue of information burglaries in the prior years was mainly at the forefront of everybody's thoughts. Knowing my attention on cybersecurity speculations, somebody asked me: Why does it continue occurring?

I'll center around one off the beaten path industry - abroad sending - for a clarification.

A "Fingers Crossed" Cybersecurity Plan

As indicated by the BBC, a private security firm named CyberKeel propelled three years back with bringing a more elevated amount of mindfulness about infections and information robbery. The appropriate response from large transportation organizations, Don't squander your chance. We're entirely protected. There's no need.

That is run of the mill. Hack assaults resemble retreats - they're not genuine until the point that one transpires.

It turns out one shipper had an infection in its PC framework that adds a programmer's ledger number each time the delivery organization's providers asked for electronic installment.

The hack extricated a few million dollars, as indicated by CyberKeel before the shipper acknowledged why its providers weren't getting paid.

The issue that crosses over into intolerability was the NotPetya ransomware assault this late spring. The goliath Danish transporting firm Maersk as of late said the hack constrained it to end tasks at 76 of its sea terminals around the globe, causing $300 million worth of interruptions to its business.

Maersk's CEO told the Financial Times that the assault was so harming "we wound up utilizing WhatsApp on our private telephones [to communicate]. It was, honestly, a significant stunning background."

The fact of the matter is, gigantic cyber hacks continue happening when PC security is not the best need for an organization.

It's likewise a key motivation behind why cybersecurity stocks will keep on being colossal champs for a considerable length of time to come.

The critical test - even now - is motivating organizations to consider the danger important.

If we claim a physical business, a home or an auto, security is dependably a need, correct? We ensure we have solid bolts on the entryways.

It doesn't keep a break-in. However, a high bolt, sustained entryways and unbreakable windows beyond any doubt make the criminals' activity significantly harder.

We pull on the entryway handle two or three times to ensure the deadbolt is set. We advise our representatives and kids to make a point to bolt the entryways when they clear out.

Why It's "Diversion On" for Cybersecurity Stocks

However - merely accepting the transportation business as one precedent - most organizations do no such thing. Sea delivering today is profoundly reliant on locally available PCs and computerization. That is the reason vessels that once required teams of handfuls in decades past would now be able to be worked with as few as 13 individuals.

But then, when a British counseling firm reviewed 2,500 vendor sailors about adrift cybersecurity, they found:

40% of boats' officers said they had cruised on a vessel tainted with a PC infection or malware.

Eighty-seven percent of boats' groups had no cybersecurity preparing.

It takes a normal of 146 days to identify a shipboard information break.

70% of shipboard information breaks go undetected.

Studies like the one above show why cybersecurity stocks will keep on riding the influx of spending in this segment, as business after business, and industry after industry, awakens to the danger.

With symmetric cryptography, a similar key is utilized for both encryption and unscrambling. A sender and a beneficiary should as of now have a mutual key that is known to both. Essential dispersion is a precarious issue and was the catalyst for creating unbalanced cryptography.

With topsy-turvy crypto, two unique keys are utilized for encryption and unscrambling. Each client in a hilter kilter cryptosystem has both an open core and a private key. The private key is kept mystery consistently, yet people in general heart might be uninhibitedly conveyed.

Information encoded with an open key may just be unscrambled with the relating private key. In this way, making an impression on John requires scrambling that message with John's public key. No one but John can unscramble the word, as just John has his private key. Any information struggled with a private key must be unscrambled with the relating open key. So also, Jane could carefully sign a message with her private key, and anybody with Jane's public key could decode the marked signal and confirm that it was in truth Jane who sent it.

Symmetric is, for the most part, quick and perfect for encoding a lot of information (e.g., a whole plate parcel or database). Awry is much slower and can scramble bits of information that are littler than the critical size (typically 2048 bits or littler). In this way, lopsided crypto is, for the most part, used to scramble symmetric encryption keys which are then used to encode considerably bigger squares of information. For computerized marks, awry crypto is, for the most part, used to encrypt the hashes of messages as opposed to whole words.

A cryptosystem accommodates overseeing cryptographic keys including age, trade, stockpiling, utilize, denial, and substitution of the keys.

What issues does cryptography explain?

A safe framework ought to give a few confirmations, for example, secrecy, trustworthiness, and accessibility of information and additionally validness and non-disavowal. At the point when utilized effectively, crypto gives these affirmations. Cryptography can guarantee the privacy and honesty of the two information in travel and also information very still. It can likewise confirm senders and beneficiaries to each other and ensure against renouncement.

Programming frameworks regularly have different endpoints, commonly numerous customers, and at least one back-end servers. These customer/server correspondences happen over systems that can't be trusted. Mail occurs over open, open systems, for example, the Internet, or private systems which might be endangered by outer aggressors or malevolent insiders.

It can ensure interchanges that navigate untrusted systems. There are two fundamental kinds of assaults that an enemy may endeavor to complete on a network. Inactive charges include an assailant just tuning in on a system portion and endeavoring to peruse touchy data as it ventures. Uninvolved costs might be on the web (in which an aggressor scrutinizes activity continuously) or disconnected (in which an assailant catches movement progressively and sees it later—maybe after investing some energy decoding it). Dynamic assaults include an aggressor mimicking a customer or server, capturing interchanges in travel, and seeing and additionally altering the substance before passing them on to their expected goal (or dropping them altogether).

The privacy and uprightness assurances offered by cryptographic conventions, for example, SSL/TLS can shield interchanges from pernicious listening in and altering. Validness securities give affirmation that clients are speaking with the frameworks as expected. For instance, would you say you are sending your web-based managing a secret account word to your bank or another person?

It can likewise be utilized to secure information very still. Information on a removable plate or in a database can be encoded to avert exposure of touchy details should the physical media be lost or stolen. What's more, it can likewise give trustworthiness assurance of information very still to recognize vindictive altering.

What are the standards?

The most critical rule to remember when utilizing cryptography is that you ought to never endeavor to outline your cryptosystem. The world's most splendid cryptographers (counting Phil Zimmerman and Ron Rivest) routinely make cryptosystems with genuine security blemishes in them. All together for a cryptosystem to be regarded as "secure," it must face extreme investigation from the security network. Never depend on security through lack of clarity or the way that assailants might not know about your framework. Keep in mind that malignant insiders and decided assailants will endeavor to assault your structure.

The main things that ought to be "mystery" with regards to a protected cryptosystem are merely the keys. Make sure to find a way to secure any keys that your frameworks utilize. Never store encryption enters in explicit content alongside the information that they obtain. This is much the same as locking your front entryway and setting the key under the doormat. It is the primary spot an aggressor will look. Here are three conventional techniques for ensuring keys (from slightest secure to generally anchor):

Store enters in a record framework and secures them with reliable access control records (ACLs). Make sure to hold fast to the central of slightest benefit.

Scramble your information encryption keys (DEKs) with a crucial second encoding key (KEK). The KEK ought to be produced utilizing secret key-based encryption (PBE). A secret key known to a negligible number of directors can be used to create a key using a calculation, for example, bcrypt, script, or PBKDF2 and used to bootstrap the cryptosystem. This evaluates the need ever to store the key decoded anyplace.

An equipment security module (HSM) is an alter safe equipment machine that can be utilized to store keys safely. The code can make API calls to an HSM to give keys when required or to perform unscrambling of information on the HSM itself.

Ensure that you utilize calculations, essential qualities, and methods of activity that comply with industry best practices. Propelled encryption standard (AES) (with 128, 192, or 256-piece keys) is the standard for symmetric encryption. RSA and circular bend cryptography (ECC) with somewhere around 2048-piece keys are the standards for lopsided encryption. Make sure to maintain a strategic distance from unreliable methods of activity, for example, AES in Electronic Codebook (ECB) mode or RSA with no cushioning.

CHAPTER SIX

HOW TO USE THE RISK MANAGEMENT FRAMEWORK FOR REQUIREMENT AND THREAT TRACEABILITY?

Cybersecurity and Information Security (InfoSec) exercises are actualized to ensure information, data, frameworks, and clients. Talented security, program and framework partners cooperate to guarantee that business destinations are met while limiting the danger of dangers where information or framework control might be lost. This misfortune might be because of robbery, catastrophic events, PC/server breakdown, unapproved or unsafe activity, or from some other dangers. Program Management and security approaches are consolidated to amplify business capacities and abilities while likewise ensuring an association. These methodologies include

Requirements Management, Risk Management, Threat Vulnerability Scanning, Continuous Monitoring, and System and Information Backups. These administration approaches require critical experience to augment results and anticipate issues that could have generally been counteracted.

Program Managers, as delegates of their organizations and customers, require the convenient conveyance of value items and administrations to tasks. Colossal experience expands item quality and execution while likewise limiting dangers. The experience encourages oversight, open joint effort, and central leadership to boost advancement, consistent quality, manageability, and the coordination of advantages and assets.

A vital Program Management concern today is that a lot of secret data is gathered, handled and put away by each substance and shared crosswise over different private and open systems to different PCs. Intensifying this worry is the quick pace of innovation, programming, norms, and various changes that the industry must keep up attention to. It is essential that this data be painstakingly overseen inside organizations and ensured to avert both the business and its clients from far-reaching, unsalvageable money related misfortune, also harm to your organization's notoriety. Securing our information and data is a moral and lawful necessity for each undertaking and requires proactive commitment to be viable.

Various Cybersecurity apparatuses and strategies are utilized to oversee hazard inside framework improvement and business tasks successfully. By need, administration, designing, and Cybersecurity exercises should proactively work inside the execution of prerequisites to boost framework capacities and abilities while additionally limiting dangers. Depend on it; the risks to our organizations, frameworks, and clients are genuine. As prerequisites are adequately recorded, so should the security controls that are expected to help moderate the known dangers to our structures.

Prerequisites and dangers are reported similarly as to guarantee traceability and repeatability. The proactive administration is expected to actualize, execute, control, test, confirm, and approve that the necessities have been met and the physical dangers have been relieved. The administration distinction is while obligations should, at last, be satisfied, dangers are overseen and alleviated on the probability and seriousness of the risk to our clients, organizations, and frameworks. Dangers are archived to demonstrate administration and relief. Reporting these prerequisites and hazards and their subtle supporting elements is the way to the proactive and repeatable exertion that is required. We trust the best methodology in doing this is to keep this administration as clear as would be prudent and as the point, my point, as expected to design, execute, and control the program or business.

Hazard Management Framework (RMF) forms are connected to the Security Controls that are found in Cybersecurity and Information Security references. These RMF exercises are all around archived and cover the accepted procedures of administration and designing. Regularly, you will see that the activities suggested of the RMF are exercises that you should as of now be doing with the unique capability. Traceability of these program and security exercises require the capacity to confirm the history and status of each security control, in any case, if the framework is being developed or in the task. Documentation by need is point by point. Traceability incorporates the different proof between prerequisite, security control, and the vital data expected to follow between necessities, security controls, techniques, approaches, plans, forms, methodology, control settings, and other data that is supposed to guarantee repeatable lifecycle improvement and operational repeatability.

Program Management and Risk Management encounter are of essential significance to overseeing necessities and hazard. An enormous and central guide of the accomplished is the Requirement Traceability Matrix (RTM) and Security Control Traceability Matrix (SCTM). The RTM and SCTM are on a fundamental level direct in reason and extension which encourages traceability and repeatability for the program. The factors of an RTM and SCTM can be fundamentally the same as and are tailorable to the necessities of the application and client. There are numerous precedents for the substance subtle elements of the RTM or SCTM, both separate however comparable reports, that may include:

1) A remarkable RTM or SCTM distinguishing proof number for every prerequisite and security control,

2) referenced ID quantities of any related things for prerequisites following,

3) a point by point, word for word depiction of the necessity or security control,

4) specialized suspicions or client require connected to the useful necessity,

5) the present status of the valuable prerequisite or security control,

6) a depiction of the capacity to the building/outline archive,

7) a representation of the specialized practical detail,

8) an image of the practical framework component(s),

9) a description of the functional programming module(s),

10) the experiment number connected to the practical prerequisite,

11) the utilitarian necessity test status and usage arrangement,

12) a depiction of the actual check archive, and

13) a different remarks section that may help to traceability.

While the substance of the RTM and SCTM are adaptable, the requirement for such devices isn't. With the unpredictability and need to shield frameworks and administrations today from different dangers, old chiefs, specialists, clients, and various experts will search for the traceability that quality and secure frameworks require.

IS YOUR BUSINESS VULNERABLE TO INFORMATION AND CYBER SECURITY RISKS?

Associations and organizations frequently work with noteworthy hazard because of an over-reliance on receptive hazard countermeasures and weakness checking devices. This hazard is of concern not just as a result of the high likelihood of assault to our IT frameworks, yet also because of the low need of data security exercises when contrasted with other operational "necessities." This complex hierarchical concern, nearly guarantees that data and cybersecurity aren't given lack until after a critical loss of data or framework accessibility happens an association. This hazard left unmanaged, subjects all partners to loss of our favored data and the extraordinary expense of framework and occurrence recuperation.

The assaults to our frameworks regularly target center mission and framework administrations to gain advantaged data and for denying access to critical administrations. Readily for our clients, and us there are chance administration arrangements that expand security and give noteworthy asset and cost investment funds all through your business improvement and operational lifecycle (NOT precisely when vulnerabilities are found). These hazard administration arrangements, once actualized, accommodate mission center and nonstop observing while additionally offsetting security prerequisites with business vision, framework functionalities, and operational abilities.

Arrangements ought to incorporate organizations possess exercises learned with operational activities to fill their own essential Information Security (IS) and cybersecurity holes. Each business, or associated gathering, has exceptional dangers that are overseen. These arrangements have guides and experienced experts that control the expense or potentially many-sided quality of expanding to an expanded security level. These accomplished experts' assistance in recognizing and tending to particular business prerequisites into approaches and plans that help the exercises required by both the mission and supporting IS (cybersecurity) norms.

The arrangements are executed utilizing different, frequently covering exercises and include: 1) Aligning the business mission, vision, objectives, destinations and IS an incentive by characterizing IS necessities mid, 2) Provide experienced industry program supervisors and IS experts that will work nearby the numerous partners, 3) Assess prerequisites and esteem, suggest arrangements, incorporate administrations, and maintain IS esteem, capacities and abilities to diminish hazard, 4) Provide esteem centered framework capacities, capacities, adaptability, and execution that enhances the mission and lessens risk to the partners, 5) Leverage IS administrations for ceaseless checking and esteem included computerization.

Hazard Management is eventually identified with numerous ventures and assignments that line up with your vision and desire for giving esteemed administrations at each level of your association. Tasks have distinct and essential stages that are consecutive; these venture stages' prosperity or disappointment specifically affect on and at last influences the achievement of the association. Is a fundamentally critical bit of numerous continuous exercises in a different and master condition. A joined program administration, frameworks designing, and IS proficient methodology will most rapidly amplify mission efficiencies while enhancing essentials expected to meet and actualize security controls. Administration and specific exercises, concentrated on mission needs, ought to take after custom fitted industry best practices to expand tasks, oversee chance and be consistent with IS security necessities.

Enhancing activities and the sustainment of is best done starting from the top, on both administration and specific levels. This application

INFORMATION SECURITY SERVICES: HOW COULD THEY HELP YOUR BUSINESS?

Data security administrations are not for the most part considered in same breath from administration counseling and are typically dispatched to the dark gap of the IT office. Notwithstanding, this is an oversight. At the point when utilized admirably, cybersecurity administrations can hugely affect business and can have a significant effect on its long-haul practicality if it turns into an objective.

The facts demonstrate this is a specialty region. Data security administrations are ordinarily the area of specific consultancies or a little office inside a considerably more significant association. PC security isn't a region that looks for the spotlight, and cybersecurity administrations must be searched out. The potential advantages for any entrepreneur are colossal.

Regardless, a consultancy firm offering cybersecurity administrations will have the pro skill expected to enable you to shield your business from programmers and insider dangers. If your business is a little one with minimal turnover, you may think it is safe from programmers. Be that as it may, numerous programmers complete their assaults not from a money-related motivating force, but instead primarily for entertainment purposes. These alleged "content kiddies" will frequently mount sharp charges against any association with a PC organize that happens to have an unguarded port open to the Internet. This is the place the data security administrations offered by a counseling organization can enable you to solidify your PC frameworks against assault, and enhance your episode reaction and recuperation techniques for use after a fruitful charge.

Nonetheless, there is a whole other world to it than just PC security. There is likewise the region of formal strategies and inside benchmarks to consider, managing the conduct of people as opposed to PCs. This, as might be normal, is substantially harder to accomplish: people seldom counsel a calculation before endeavoring a standard undertaking. By the by, data security administrations can establish the framework of a full Information Security Management System (ISMS), which incorporates the human component and also the specialized, and which will ensure the business on all levels and in all divisions.

And also, the clear hacking situation, digital security administrations from a perceived counseling firm can likewise have an impact in figuring a Business Continuity Plan (BCP) for your business. Calamity Recovery, or the rebuilding of registering workstations and framework, is a fundamental piece of the BCP, which might be activated by either a catastrophic event or a consider assault. This is another zone where authority learning and experience can be precious since just the extremely most magnificent associations will have the assets essential to build up their very own in-house ability in a territory that isn't called upon consistently.

Furthermore, data security administrations can spare your business a considerable measure of time and cash. A very much planned and redid ISMS can streamline the procedures associated with actualizing security controls, observing their task, and auditing the proceeded with the requirement for everyone. Rather than constant divided putting out fires, your CISO will have the capacity to actualize the fundamental protects in a controlled and timely way. This can prompt a sparing in time and cash - also a decrease of the pressure experienced by the CISO.

In a rundown, accordingly, data security administrations - while frequently disregarded - can conceivably offer a lot of advantage for a business of any size.

Why It's Critical to Keep Your Software Updated

Programming is all over the place; we can't survive without it. For the individuals who experienced childhood in the 80's and 90's recollect the energy for work area equipment, swapping out RAM, Hard Drives, CPU's and so on it was fun and simple to give your PC some genuinely necessary lift. Today, except for cell phones, equipment has been assigned to the rearward sitting arrangement and programming is up front in numerous structures. The layers of programming keep on developing - we currently have programming running as firewalls and virtual machines supplanting hundred of physical equipment boxes. We can live amazing the product in our lives and in our business surroundings, which is the reason it is so critical to stay up with the latest.

On the off chance that I place this in the point of view of Cybersecurity, the assault surface has become in the course of the last 10-15 years, and it's not backing off. This gives an assailant more vectors, or openings, to assault you or your business. Anyplace you have programming running, regardless of whether you know it or not, turns into a gap that could be misused. Does everybody cherish those wifi-associated "secure" entryway locks for your home, so advantageous right? Beyond any doubt, they can be, yet they can likewise be hacked in minutes with negligible exertion - there is a 42 page how-to direct from Defcon, an association of moral programmers, demonstrating the world how simple it is.

So what does this mean for you and your business? It implies programming must be stayed up with the latest as fast and as securely as possible. This diminishes the assault surface, giving an eventual criminal programmer, fewer purposes of shortcoming to abuse. You would prefer not to be in the press. A portion of the most significant organizations, the most recent being Equifax, turned into the focal point of media consideration all since they neglected to fix a system part adequately. We separate it for the individuals who need to take in more about this specific precedent - Equifax Data Breach 2017.

Motivations to stay up with the latest:

SECURITY! For the above-noted reasons... try not to make it simple for an assailant to misuse a known defenselessness.

Soundness - Generally, programming refreshes not just decrease security gaps that could cut your frameworks down, yet they increment strength, so they are more reluctant to break for some other reason.

Similarity - New programming likes to sit on new programming, if you need to stay aware of the occasions, you'll have to stay up with the latest.

Testing will be your closest companion - dependably test your product on non-mission necessary equipment and in test or non-generation situations. You need to stay up with the latest. However, you would prefer not to break whatever else all the while, so test, test, test, at that point convey.

DIGITAL SECURITY CONSULTANTS: WHO ARE THEY AND WHAT DO THEY DO?

A digital security advisor more often than not has extensive experience with either PC security or data security principles. The sort of aptitude required is exceedingly specific and presently not exceptionally far-reaching. The administrations given by cybersecurity experts can have a genuine effect on an association's general security pose and may anticipate or possibly moderate future attacks by programmers or certifiable fraudsters.

Digital security is only one a player in the more extensive field of data security, which likewise covers physical resources and dangers, and individuals related variables. In any case, in the present setting of developing hazards to the basic national foundation, (for example, control plants) from specific nations, it is the "digital" some portion of the term that is taking an undeniably prominent. The facts confirm that most associations won't be in danger from invasions by state-supported specialists. Notwithstanding, they may at present be the objective of a pioneering novice programmer, and it is here that digital security experts can have an influence.

The expert may review the association's current level of IT security, calling attention to territories where there are high-chance vulnerabilities (for instance, site pages where a username and secret word are transmitted decoded). Numerous vulnerabilities originate from old programming that has not been refreshed to the most recent fix level. For this situation, just updating the product will resolve the circumstance. In different cases, while the outcome might be present with the most recent security patches, there might be a need to reconfigure it to change the settings. The defenselessness sweeps and infiltration tests did by digital security advisors will uncover these circumstances and the sky is the limit from there, empowering the association to settle the vulnerabilities previously programmers find them.

A cybersecurity expert can offer significantly more than defenselessness appraisals, offering additionally particular consultancy administrations to build up an arrangement for updating an association's data security. This sort of administration is completely custom fitted to the customer as opposed to depending on off-the-rack strategies and reports and considers the customer association's state of mind to hazard and business needs. It can incorporate PC security, as well as training and mindfulness measures to raise the profile of security among representatives or accomplices. Numerous digital security advisors can likewise aid the procedure of confirmation to ISO 27001, the worldwide data security standard.

Cybersecurity is an irregular zone of business consultancy administrations, including as it does both exceptionally specialized skill and furthermore learning of individuals and systems. It is incompletely thus that digital security experts are both unprecedented and exceedingly looked for after, with the capacity to have a genuine effect on any association that utilizes their administrations.

CYBER SECURITY NEWS: 4 WEBSITES TO KEEP YOUR BUSINESS SAFE

Ever ponder where we IT parents get our mystery digital security news? Goodness, it's no place extraordinary. We all get together every couple a long time at Area51 and get our briefings straight from the men dressed in dark and their reptile individual's overlords running the Underground White House. In all seriousness, we remain over digital security news by instructing ourselves through dependable assets both on and disconnected.

Where you scan for data relies on your industry. However, these four sites can give a wellspring of IT security information to anybody, paying little heed to a trade.

Infragard.org

Infragard is a joint effort between the FBI and the private part devoted to sharing data and insight that can brace organizations against cyber-attacks. The participation is free, and you can limit the data you get to your particular industry area - from vitality, back, and human services to assembling, nourishment administrations, and past.

When you enroll, you will likewise get messages with extraordinary data sharing brilliant tips and breaking digital security news. Also, as a part, you even can remain up to date about future cybersecurity occasions that relate to your industry and district. Unquestionably justified regardless of the enlistment.

Databreaches.net

Databreaches.net is fundamentally an online rundown of useful examples. As a guard dog for the most recent digital security news, you can expect refreshes from information breaks substantial and little. Need to find out about the extent of information breaks and the procedures utilized by digital hoodlums? You get the majority of the subtle elements expected to enable you to gain from the exercises of large brands and your industry peers.

Updates come a few times day by day and cover unfurling stories as they occur. This is just one more indication of how important an educated and consistently developing IT security methodology is for any business.

Security Bloggers Network

Need to get notification from IT specialists about digital security news, yet tired of perusing many websites? The Security Bloggers Network goes about as a total and unites assets from over the web. Everything from industry outlines to the most recent digital security patterns and debates is combined in one spot.

IT Security Guru

IT Security Guru is a network of IT parents that give primary data to general society and their individuals. They have a "trick of the week" refresh, keeping individuals mindful of the most recent ways that digital offenders are profiting by IT vulnerabilities.

Likewise, you would prefer not to be on their main ten lists. They take a gander at a portion of the most significant and most essential stories from over the web and not very many of them are complimenting stories of IT security best practices.

Google Stresses Using Strong Passwords

There is no denying to the way that there are a couple of deficiencies in the Google benefits however since passwords remain the essential methods for online validation. That is the reason Google is endeavoring all endeavors to ensure that clients passwords don't get effortlessly crushed. The National Cybersecurity Awareness Month is going on, and Google is underlining that clients ought to pick robust and extraordinary passwords for their online administrations. There are a few thousand clients of Windows Live Hotmail, alongside a few clients of Gmail and Yahoo Mail, need new passwords.

The guidance for clients of Hotmail, Gmail, and Yahoo Mail to change their passwords following the presentation of a few thousand Hotmail certifications on a Web webpage. Microsoft trusts that the performance was the possible aftereffect of a phishing trick. Reports have surfaced that some Gmail and Yahoo Mail account data was likewise uncovered. So it's prudent for clients who may have entered account data in a phishing site ought to instantly pick an alternate secret phrase.

Michael Santerre, who is the Google shopper tasks relate, exhorts utilizing one of a kind password for each site. He proposes choosing an expression and using the central letter of each word in the appearance or some variety of that as a secret word, in a perfect world with different characters included to make it more secure. It would be sufficiently insightful to pick the passwords that ought to be a blend of letters, numbers, and images to limit the danger of lexicon assaults, by which cybercriminals utilize projects to attempt each word in a word reference database as a potential password. This is profound.

Utilizing individual data as a secret key ought to be a flat out no-no. Since that data can frequently be effortlessly gotten to on informal organization profiles and amassed from other online sources.This is interesting, however, is genuine Stay far from the names of pets or kids, birthday celebrations, telephone numbers, addresses, or something like that. That is a cake stroll for cybercriminals to figure. Another bit of cool guidance is to keep away from leaving passwords on notes alongside your PC. It might sound clear, yet it's a typical issue.

At last, Google focuses on that your secret phrase recuperation data ought to be dependent upon date. Its evident that once you pick a mind-boggling secret key, you may overlook it, and you don't need the secret word to reset email heading off to a relinquished email account or to somebody who may misuse the chance to capture your record.

THE FIGHT AGAINST CYBER THREATS REQUIRES A DOSE OF COMMON SENSE

It is generally comprehended that presence of mind isn't normal. It is all the more baffling when the methodologies utilized by a few associations to keep digital assaults from significant business resources do not have the use of the presence of mind. This part records ongoing investigations on the frequencies at which a few long associations examine their systems to recognize vulnerabilities and enhance their security act. While zero-day assaults (malware brought into the internet for which countermeasures have not been produced) comprise around 13% of the considerable number of vulnerabilities (Ponemon Institute, 2014); the staying 87% is notable, and countermeasures exist for avoiding them. The part additionally distinguishes a portion of the complacencies of a few associations in battling digital dangers and offers a few recommendations for ensuring the data and correspondence frameworks that help both government and private associations from digital assaults.

Current apparatuses that caution the IT staff to react to data on digital dangers are deficient in addressing the considerable volume and complexity of present-day digital threats. Along these lines astute digital security arrangements that can anticipate and stop hazards on the systems are expected to address the restrictions of conventional risk administration devices. Current endeavors to anchor the internet have brought about producing substantial open databases of vulnerabilities at NIST and Symantec. In any case, access to vulnerabilities databases is only the initial phase in overseeing dangers to the systems, yet it won't decrease the recurrence and harms caused by digital assaults except if arrange executives are furnished with electronic security instruments. Those endeavors to anchor the internet are not being helped because few associations and buyers are ease back to apply distributed security refreshes.

The need to center around computerization as opposed to depending on human capital: Scanning the systems creates a large measure of vulnerabilities that must be broken down with a specific end goal to pick up knowledge about the system also called Situational Awareness. Just distributing the most helpless hubs and cautioning the framework executive to react isn't viable. It looks terrible to anticipate that the human cerebrum will process more than 300 vulnerabilities and apply essential countermeasures day by day without expecting a mind solidify. Rather than mourning on the deficiency of faculty or cybersecurity specialists, a lot of assets should be dedicated to processing robotization. Instead of depending on people to perform entrance testing after the vulnerabilities have been distinguished, devices that consequently create conceivable assault ways and avert assaults on significant business resources ought to be the core interest.

Resistance in Depth: The idea of barrier in-depth is broadly comprehended by cybersecurity experts and ought to be connected. To secure or solidify every hub on the system, it is essential to utilize no less than five procedures. I) Employ progressive enemy of infection programming that can purify both known and obscure malware. 2) Control the utilization of specific gadgets, (for example, debilitating the blue tooth on your workstation) in broad daylight particularly at air terminals and Coffee shops; 3) Encrypt the hard drive and the media to secure put away information (exercises from Sony and OPM); 4) Control applications to avert un-confided in changes (e.g., SQL infusion); and 5) Patch administration to guarantee that the framework is running the most current programming. Protecting in Depth is likewise called Host-Based Access Control in specific quarters. Once the host has been secured, determined endeavors ought to be made to shield the system (i.e., associated hubs).

Finishing up Remarks

Relatively consistently, we read about the vulnerabilities of the legislature and private systems and the noteworthy expense to the economy, protected innovation and security of people. Many set up organizations and government offices exhaust large measure of assets to create and convey cybersecurity instruments, yet the assaults proceed. Why one may inquire. While we as a whole comprehend that the issue is hard, there are some essential advances that we have to take to address the issue. Week by week examining of the system accept that the programmer does not endeavor to infiltrate the system less frequently. It is safe to say that we are agreeable to enable the programmers to wander the system for seven days? Controlling access to necessary resources require more than 2 or even 3-factor validation. Encoding the information with extremely solid encryption calculation to make it exceptionally troublesome for the hoodlums to utilize stolen information bodes well. Rather than mourning on the deficiency of cybersecurity experts (which is valid), center around canny computerization to lessen the level of exertion for playing out a few daily assignments. Those means are what this creator call sound judgment approaches.

CHAPTER SEVEN

A NEW MODEL FOR CYBER SECURITY

Advanced interchanges related to the utilization of the cutting edge web have developed exponentially to the indicate that impart carefully has turned into a crucial feature of regular day to day existence. From cell phones to netbooks to email, web journals and online entrances, the exchange and trade of electronic information controls the manner in which many interfaces with one another and convey both by and by and for business. Presently with the present pattern moving towards "cloud" processing where each of the people or organizations keep critical records put away and got to on the web or in the "cloud," digital security has now turned into the primary need of many.

Strategies to ensure information as encryption, antivirus programming, firewalls, and access passwords have been around some time before the advanced information unrest, yet shockingly none of such have developed as compelling security answers for the suit the cutting edge methods of electronic correspondence. Gadgets which can interface with the worldwide information system or the Internet, have turned out to be progressively littler and shrewder. For instance, with only a cutting-edge cell phone, a man can get to their email, present reports on web journals, and access individual or corporate records all through the web.

The standard security approach in the past has been founded on the model to confine get to utilizing firewall frameworks or identify interruptions as infections using mark based examining structures. Every such arrangement depends on the idea to limit, channel, cover up and constrain access to information. A firewall, for instance, obtains its name from "flame retardent dividers" which are intended to make safe zones where fire can't pass as a result of the material from which they are developed. For this situation, any external access that has not been esteemed important to an interior or the open system is considered fire and just blocked. Antivirus arrangements and the Virus signature demonstrate have additionally demonstrated lacking given the pivot time required to refresh signature documents and the measure of assets such frameworks use to check 1000's of records. It resembles the idea of sending the police to everyone's house in a city of a great many individuals to attempt and find where the miscreants are stowing away. With present-day PCs containing a few 1000 documents, and the regularly changing relatively polymorphic nature of current infections, the mark based examining model never again is down to earth.

The issues with the present methodologies are with the undeniably broad utilization of advanced systems; there has never been any strategy in which to powerfully refresh firewalls or mark databases to oblige for new sorts of access and dangers. Daily there are new applications which are always getting to be important for individuals to access computerized administrations adequately and similarly new risks. The present security display was never intended to be an answer that decides immediately between great action and terrible. Truth be told it limits the opportunity of the whole gathering to shield from the potential dangers of a couple. A valuable security framework must have the capacity to permit and keep up access to the group and afterward just constraining or denying access to those exercises that are out of line with the full standard of activities.

Every security procedure carries with it an expense of proprietorship, and for the most part firewalls, antivirus programming, VPN systems, and access control techniques serve more to confine access to advanced computerized systems that ensure them. Framework heads and corporate IT security chiefs can never again possibly take after the confine everything model since at last, they are only limiting real access and to a significant degree constraining the capacity of their clients to take full preferred standpoint of the advanced data upheaval and doing little to counteract real "programmers" or unapproved access to their systems.

A genuinely viable digital security arrangement must be as robust and adaptable as the score of each changing applications and computerized administrations and advanced access gadgets being utilized. It is not anymore an achievable model to limit everything, or filter everything, as this serves to thwart clients from exploiting the expanded efficiency and power brought by the cutting edge advanced systems and web and is a gigantic utilization of figuring assets.

The cybersecurity security show for information systems can be characterized as something which ensures information and information frameworks by denying access to unapproved clients, forestalling downtime of approved administrations by unapproved exercises (Denial of Service assaults), and safeguarding the general useful condition of a strength of an advanced system at 99%.

1)Protecting of information and information frameworks from unapproved get to

As more data is being put away online as financial data, charge card numbers, characterized reports and data that can't fall into unapproved hands, information assurance is the best worry of cybersecurity. Shockingly there have been numerous well-known security breaks of critical information as a vast number of credit numbers stolen, to a robbery of corporate competitive innovations and even worries of outside nations recovering national security data by the utilization of trojans and other interruption strategies.

Strategies for interruption incorporate.

The introducing of indirect access arrange interruption applications covered up in or camouflaged as specific applications that enter inside a system by approved clients incidentally opening tainted messages or sites.

Savage power assaults, where common client names and weak passwords are misused by frameworks that attempt a vast number of mixes of username, secret word sets to get entrance.

Endeavors in working frameworks as Microsoft windows that permits a safe or approved administration to be misused by discovered defects in the programming projects plan.

Robbery or rupture of interior systems by representatives or people regularly approved with enabled access to the frameworks, or who hold access to specific zones whereby inward snooping they can discover passwords and auth codes to anchor regions. (Notes left on work areas, PCs left signed in to anchor zones.

Presenting information to outer rupture by setting archives on USB pen drives and workstations with a specific end goal to give such details in gatherings outside of the system. Ordinarily, workers put a report on a USB pen that is for an introduction at a remote area, yet they happen likewise to have secure records inconsequential to the present gathering which got left on their USB. At that point they put their pen drive in an outsider PC keeping in mind the end goal to exhibit 1 archive, not realizing that specific PC has a trojan which rapidly duplicates the majority of the information on their USB to an unapproved three party area.

2)Preventing downtime of approved administrations by unapproved exercises

Savage power assaults, scanners, and dissent of administration assaults can cause a system, its servers and primary access switches, to be conveyed down to the point that the system is not any more usable in any shape. Such assaults cause great harm and downtime to systems every day. The capacity to recognize such charges and cut them off at the source most distant far from the center system and its administrations are vital to the general strength of a robust cybersecurity program.

3) Preserving the general practical condition of the wellbeing of an advanced system.

Saving the strength of an advanced system isn't merely in the counteractive action of assaults and unapproved movement yet additionally in the protection of center administrations, and information gets to that its approved clients rely on. It's anything but a practical answer for stop an assault or counteracts potential charges by likewise avoiding or constraining approved access. A cybersecurity arrangement must have the capacity to confine and avert costs and breaks to its honesty by in the meantime not restricting or denying access to its assets by approved clients.

It was evident from the full range of ways that security can be ruptured in information systems, and the mind-boggling reliance on such arrangements that the present security techniques are not just no longer sufficient to ensure such systems, yet themselves serve to cause greater security issues additionally and system get to points. A critical need has emerged to change the present method of the way to deal with cybersecurity and make another powerful model that can always adjust to the regularly changing requirements for securing information systems.

Another IDS show must be made that needs to hold fast to the accompanying objectives:

The objective of any IDS framework must be to save the honesty of the system in which it ensures and enable such an order to work in its optimal working state at 99.99%. An IDS framework must be lightweight and progressively conveyed. An IDS framework can't itself turn into another interruption and must not defy the chief norm by involving the systems uprightness in utilizing excessively figuring and system assets in its endeavors to secure the network.

An IDS framework must have the capacity to adjust to a consistently changing condition continually and self-refresh its mark records in light of developing dangers. An IDS framework must not require broad hands-on assets to frequently refresh its mark records and require a manual check that the risks it distinguished are real and not false. An IDS framework must have the capacity to at the same time secure the system against assaults, unapproved utilize and downtime, without averting nor constraining system access and utilization of system assets to approved customers. It must be unpretentious consistently and save the system in an open state where its center administrations and assets are 99.99% accessible to the methods supported clients while distinguishing, segregating and averting unapproved action.

Genuinely just research in proactive barrier components will hold helpfulness in ensuring the computerized systems of now and later on.

Intuitiveness and reliance on gadgets are expanding with time as the idea of IoT (web of things) fortifies with time. While IoT seeks after most great accommodation for people and organizations, it has its related difficulties as well. The more entwined the advanced gadgets turn into, the higher the danger of cybersecurity dangers will be. Little, medium or extensive, your presentation to actual web dangers does not rely upon the measure of your business. If you are an independent venture, you are presented to similarly the same number of threats as expansive endeavors. The drawback for private companies is that they are not as ready as large organizations against digital dangers.

Things being what they are, how are cyber security dangers are expanding with time and what sort of hazards confronting independent companies today? Investigate the numerous ways digital risks represent a threat to independent companies.

The Ever-expanding Count of Cyber Security Risks

· The BYOD Issue

BYOD (bring your gadget) is a trait of IT consumerization. To remain profitable and proficient in the meantime, an ever-increasing number of organizations are enabling their workers to utilize their very own gadgets to access and use corporate information. A case of this would be a laborer using his tablet to open organization's worker related archive store or a representative getting to work messages from his cell phone. Except if you have strict arrangements and models set for your BYOD usage, your business could be in danger of being tainted by malware originating from clients' gadgets.

· Software Update Delays

Do you ever ask why organizations are so unyielding at making their clients refresh to the most up to date programming variant? This is a result of the more established adaptations of similar programming, application, module, and so forth are available to dangers of digital assaults. With private ventures depending on different forms, web applications and modules for smooth site activities, database work, on-start security, and so forth they must be additional watchful at refreshing them all. Any non-refreshed programming or application is an open window for web criminals to hop into your framework.

· Internal Threats

You must be additional watchful while approving access to any of your representatives to your system and database. A significant number of the assaults on large organizations in the past have been purportedly executed by "inside men." Sometimes the dangers from your representatives are not purposeful yet somewhat honest. The approved individual may approach their record and neglected to log out while leaving the station. Some third individual would then be able to exploit the circumstance and cause harm to the framework.

· Sophisticated Phishing Scams

This is a typical issue with private ventures as they don't have strict conventions for workers to take after before opening messages or web-based life joins. While phishing trick has been around for a period, the new type of this trick is called stick phishing. In this sort of assault, the con artist sends email from a delivery that appears to the beneficiary as known and familiar. This tricks the individual into tapping on the connection and letting an unsafe malware (a ransomware best case scenario) enter the framework.

· Lack of Cyber Security Knowledge

Now and then, the issue isn't being set up to confront a problem. This is a typical case with numerous private companies where proprietors and overseers are under the impressions that cybercriminals won't assault them-for what reason would they? They don't understand the best part of cybercriminals, i.e., they don't trust in separation. One of the primary markers of the absence of cybersecurity learning at a work environment is when representatives pick the standard, unsurprising and straightforward passwords for their entrance focus to the organization's framework.

What Small Businesses Have to Do to Counter These Threats

· Set Policies with a BYOD Approach

If you need to take after a BYOD approach to your working environment, you better archive arrangements and directions about it. Make your representatives read these manuals deliberately, so they comprehend what measures and necessities they need to meet before they carry their gadgets into the workplace. For workers that need to get to your framework from remote areas, set up a protected VPN.

· Gives Employees Cyber Security Training

They won't know except if you let them know, so make cybersecurity-related preparing a piece of your enlisting procedure. Make web security related inquiries a few your meetings. Advise your workers to log out of their records and PCs while leaving stations. Request that they have robust passwords. Encourage them with applications to recollect those passwords as well as produce irregular and troublesome passwords. Disclose to them why such estimates matter and what the results of not conforming to the directions can be.

· Take Professional IT Help

Go for outsourced oversaw administrations or contract your very own IT experts to deal with the security-related issues. An outsourced benefit or the inside IT group will set up a whole framework comprising of arrangements, equipment, and programming advancements to shield your database from digital dangers as well as react in time if you get assaulted in any case.

· Give Authorized Accesses Wisely and Monitor Them

You can offer access to touchy organization data and the framework to just a chosen few workers. When you give them access to the frame, concede them only the authorizations as indicated by their jobs. Furthermore, have an observing framework to watch out for the exercises of these workers. Moreover, erase the records or change the passwords of files that are never again being used because the representatives they were made to have left the organization.

· Choose Third Party Services Wisely

Have legitimate gatherings and interviews before you buy into any outsider administrations. To maintain a business in the present advanced age, you need to buy into numerous stages or applications as administrations, e.g., cloud CRM. You need to make sure that you are picking an industry-perceived and dependable accomplice. They should have the correct safety efforts taken to ensure their framework as well as all of the data that goes on their cloud stage from your databases.

Bear in mind the security of your site among this. Notwithstanding your databases, inner programming, applications utilized by representatives, and so forth you need to refresh your site modules and applications in time as well.

Entirely Enforce a Multi-Tiered IT Security Plan for ALL Staff

As new dangers emerge, it is essential to stay up with the latest to secure your business. Your worker handbook needs to incorporate a multi-layered IT security plan made up of strategies for which all staff, including officials, administration and even the IT division are considered responsible.

Adequate Use Policy - Specifically demonstrate what is allowed versus what is denied to shield the corporate frameworks from superfluous introduction to hazard. Incorporate assets, for example, interior and outside email utilize, internet-based life, web perusing (counting good programs and sites), PC frameworks, and downloads (regardless of whether from an online source or glimmer drive). This approach ought to be recognized by each representative with a mark to imply they comprehend the desires put forward in the strategy.

Private Data Policy - Identifies models of information your business considers secret and how the data ought to be taken care of. This data is frequently the sort of documents which ought to be consistently supported up and are the objective for some cybercriminal exercises.

Email Policy - E-mail can be a helpful technique for passing on data any way the composed record of correspondence likewise is a wellspring of obligation should it enter the wrong hands. Having an email strategy makes sure rules for all sent and got messages and incorporations which might be utilized to obtain to the organization arrange.

BYOD/Telecommuting Policy - The Bring Your Device (BYOD) strategy covers cell phones and also organize get to use to interface with organization information remotely. While virtualization can be an excellent thought for some organizations, it is significant for staff to comprehend the dangers of advanced mobile phones and unbound Wi-Fi present.

Remote Network and Guest Access Policy - Any entrance to the system not explicitly made by your IT group ought to take after strict rules to control known dangers. At the point when visitors visit your business, you might need to contract their entrance to outbound web utilize just for instance and add other safety efforts to anybody getting to the organization's system remotely.

Episode Response Policy - Formalize the procedure the representative would follow on account of a digital occurrence. Consider situations, for example, a lost or stolen workstation, a malware assault or the representative falling for a phishing plan and giving subtle classified elements to an unapproved beneficiary. The quicker your IT group is informed of such occasions, the speedier their reaction time can be to ensure the security of your classified resources.

System Security Policy - Protecting the honesty of the corporate system is a fundamental part of the IT security plan. Has an arrangement set up indicating specific rules to anchor the system framework including the methodology to introduce, benefit, keep up and supplant all on location hardware? Also, this arrangement may incorporate procedures around secret word creation and capacity, security testing, cloud reinforcements, and related equipment.

Leaving Staff Procedures - Create standards to deny access to all sites, contacts, email, secure building passages, and other corporate association focuses instantly upon resignation or end of a worker in spite of regardless of whether you trust they old any pernicious goal towards the organization.

Preparing is certifiably not a One Time Thing; Keep the Conversation Going.

Representative digital security mindfulness preparing significantly lessens the danger of falling prey to a phishing email, getting a type of malware or ransomware that locks up access to your vital records, spill data using an information break and a developing number of mortal digital dangers that are released every day.

Untrained workers are the best danger to your information security plan. Preparing once won't be sufficient to change the dangerous propensities they have gotten throughout the years. Consistent discussions need to occur to guarantee collaboration to effectively search for the notice indications of suspicious connections and messages and how to deal with recently creating circumstances as they arise. Steady updates about the most recent dangers and authorization of your IT security plan makes sole obligation and trust in how to deal with episodes to confine presentation to an assault.

Preparing Should Be Both Useful Personal AND Professional to Stick

Make consistent chances to share local news about information ruptures and investigate distinctive cyberattack strategies amid a lunch and learn. Here and there the ideal approach to expanding consistency is to hit up close and personal by making preparing individual. Odds are your workers are similarly as ignorant about their own IT security and usual tricks as they are about the security dangers they posture to your business.

Develop this thought by stretching out an encouragement to teach their whole families about how to shield themselves from cybercrime amid a twilight occasion. Consider covering points with the end goal that may speak to a scope of age gatherings, for example, how to control the protection and security settings via web-based networking media, web-based gaming, and so on and how to perceive the risk indications of somebody phishing for individual data or cash both by means of email and telephone calls. Seniors and youthful kids are particularly powerless against such abuse.

Try not to Make a Hard Situation Harder; Remember you WANT warnings announced.

Making eternal security preparing a need will incredibly diminish rehash blunders and avert numerous avoidable assaults, anyway ruins occur. It tends to be extremely humiliating and a stun to one's pride to recognize their blunder and report contribution in a potential security break. Your first sense might be to scold and shout. However, this would be a genuine oversight. Resisting the urge to panic and gathered is the way to the trust required for workers to come to you immediately, while they feel they're generally powerless.

Therefore, treat each report with gratefulness and prompt mindfulness. Regardless of whether the alarm ends up being a false alert or a real emergency, abstain from criticizing the representative for their misstep irrespective of how red your face may move toward becoming.

At the point when the circumstance is under control, accept an open the door to express gratitude toward them for detailing the case with the goal that it very well may be taken care of fittingly. Keep in mind it makes a great deal of strength to advance up when you know you were to be faulted. Help the representative comprehend what to pay particular mind to next time is it was something that could have been counteracted, for example, a client blunder.

Digital Training Recap

Execute a Multi-Tiered IT Security Plan Strictly Enforced for ALL Staff

Preparing is certifiably not a One Time Thing;

Prop the Conversation Up

Preparing Should Be Both Useful Personal AND
Professional to Stick

Try not to Make a Hard Situation Harder; Remember you
WANT warnings announced.

Tie National is Your Nationwide Technology Partner -
Providing Outsourced IT Solutions, Managed Services, and
Business Technology Since 2003.

Sun Tzu, the Chinese military general, strategist, and
thinker said that in the event that you know your
adversaries and identify yourself, you won't be
jeopardized in a hundred fights; in the fact that you don't
have the foggiest idea about your foes yet do know
yourself, you will win one and lose one; in the fact that you
don't have the foggiest idea about your enemies nor
yourself, you will be risked in eSun Tzu, the Chinese
military general, strategist, and thinker said that in the
event that you know your adversaries and identify

yourself, you won't be jeopardized in a hundred fights; in the fact that you don't have the foggiest idea about your foes yet do know yourself, you will win one and lose one; in the fact that you don't have the foggiest idea about your opponents nor yourself, you will be risked in every fight.

To meet the security requests of the 21st-century associations are progressively perceiving their interconnectivity and relationship with the extreme condition. The outer situation consistently makes requests and makes openings expecting organizations to comprehend and adjust in like manner. Any move made by an association likewise results in the possibility of changes inside the extreme condition.

Numerous components impact an association's level of defenselessness to security chance. There are the more common factors, for example, the business working model, business execution and the association's history and the inexorably persuasive outer specialists including clients, intrigue or weight gatherings, networks and the media that are all themselves powerless to impact. The social obligation profile of an association for instance regardless of whether real or saw can fundamentally build the possibility of dangers to the security of a business.

To give the profundity and expansiveness of security essential to ensure an association requires a security procedure that expands on existing work on, fusing a more significant amount of comprehension to set up why those issuing or completing a danger have taken the choice to do as such from the setting of their condition. Utilizing this data and working related to strong organizations it is conceivable to impact and co-deliver results that diminish or expel the risk.

The decision of those speaking to risk can be seen as the communication of three angles; the level of self-intrigue, enthusiastic decision and the social standards of the individual or gathering. The idea of the risk might be proactive, for example, an antagonistic organization in the quest for a particular goal or objective, or receptive as far as an office reacting to a business change or proposition.

Business Diplomacy offers a forward-looking, proactive system to connect individually or in a roundabout way with offices to determine, break down or redirect the risk.

Business Diplomacy spins around the recognizable proof of geopolitical and social factors that can influence an organization's tasks, both at home and abroad, and the expansive scope of legislative and non-administrative partners who can shape how those elements affect on the organization. It utilizes this investigation to help create systems of data and impact among the key partners. These systems are like this used to develop "alliances of the eager" to advance and ensure the organization's business advantages. The methods can likewise be utilized to confine or disturb threatening partners or alliances of partners plan on harming the organization.

On account of cybersecurity, a Business Diplomacy driven methodology would distinguish those people or gatherings who speak to danger or may design dispatch an assault against the organization and their inspiration. This procedure would be bolstered by insight, for example, the different information scratching innovations that permit internet checking of chatrooms, web-based life and different wellsprings of data about any potential digital assailant's aims. The investigation would likewise recognize those legislative and non-administrative partners who might be more steady of the organization. Contingent upon the result from the study, the organization, would create methodologies, for example, disturbance, separation, training or redirection, for instance:

A disturbance methodology would either expect to diminish the danger through the exchange, i.e., to disseminate or resolve the contention or it would look to undermine the limit of the digital aggressors to complete an assault

A methodology of segregation would center around the inspirations of the digital assailants. Working with to a great extent non-administrative partners who to some degree share the motivations of the eventual digital aggressors, however not their strategies, the organization would look to separate the digital assailants inside their very own locale, expanding weight on them from their associates not to assault the organization.

A training system whereby the organization would build up an open discretion methodology to produce a political and social condition in which an assault would have neither rhyme nor reason

At long last, a system of preoccupation would utilize the systems to persuade the digital assailants to occupy their consideration far from the organization. Redirection will probably turn into a noteworthy cybersecurity procedure for the 21st century with organizations effectively seeking after this with NGOs, e.g., BP and Greenpeace.

The selection of a more forward-looking methodology consolidating Business Diplomacy will empower associations to develop multi-dimensional, arranged connections and relieve security hazards that exist in an undeniably unpredictable business condition.

The 21st century holds numerous difficulties for both private and open part associations. The mix of multiplication of worldwide supply chains, expanded disturbance in the global condition and strain to change challenges even the most experienced organizations. Many existing associations are currently working universally or on account of new organizations are worldwide from the origin. The global condition speaks to specialists that are not inside the control of the association but instead may have an immediate or backhanded effect on choices, exercises and the general achievement of the business.

The Cyber Domain: A Shared and Global Opportunity

The multifaceted nature and danger of the digital space

We are sharing data about the digital space, yet neither on the critical scale nor speed required. We are not managing conventional armed forces despite what might be expected, but rather awry dangers of exceedingly talented and smart people or groups with the capacity to do enormous harm. A moderately little speculation and a modest number of individuals can perpetrate unending harm at lightning speed. No principles administer this common danger that crosses effectively from singular protection to country states without imperative. To address this, the U.S. government recognizes the tremendousness of this hazard by building up the digital risk as a different area notwithstanding land, ocean, air, and space.

The hazard is huge. Regardless of whether we by and by executing business over the Internet or not, digital hoodlums may deliver our restorative chronicles, void our financial balances, and demolish our FICO assessments. Our economies and necessary frameworks rely on the Internet. Sharp digital wizards can utilize any bit of innovation with an IP deliver to harm our basic foundation, thump out dams and influence frameworks, take cash from private and open budgetary establishments, wreak destruction with our supply chains, and, harm our PC systems. Digital hoodlums and country states have stolen many measures of protected innovation national safeguard mysteries.

Not understanding who, what, and where the most qualified assets exist before a digital danger happens looks at to "flipping through the business repository" to discover who can help us afterward.

Clashes between people in general and separate divisions are much more impossible to miss to the digital area. Citizens subsidize the administration's business to secure. Governments grapple with security, title experts, guidelines and arrangement issues. The private segment tries to turn a benefit and ensure upper hands, reacting to government's solicitations or surrendering, frequently thinking that its difficult to manage government administration. The private part gripes that administration is unwilling to impart insight to industry, while the industry is unwilling to reveal to the government in light of worries about obligation and the conceivable presentation of restrictive data to contenders.

President Barack Obama and other government authorities have guaranteed industry officials that the organization's way to deal with Cybersecurity would be founded on motivations for collaboration as opposed to on control. However, some administrative specialist may be essential to get a compelling level of cooperation. At last, the private part will probably need to acknowledge some significant government control on Cybersecurity, setting up measures of training and baselines of security we can authorize.

Nobody is happy with existing conditions, and the ghost of the National Security Agency or the Cyber Command expecting control of the country's basic framework raises genuine worries about fundamental freedoms and protection.

The chance

We have shared hazard and shared weakness as people, networks, countries, and the world network. First off, numerous individuals value the requirement for worldwide organization among government and the private-segment and have made noteworthy strides toward that path. For the best-shared advantage, why not address the whole range of intricacy from a comprehensive and fair-minded viewpoint?

Why not expand on the precedents of inventive reasoning in the digital space? Making noteworthy open doors in the Cybersecurity space for the two sides, the Security Innovation Network (SINET) bolstered by the Department of Homeland Security Science and Technology Directorate, encourages consciousness of imaginative beginning period and developing development organizations. Driven by Chairman Robert Rodriguez, its controlling board of trustees incorporates a comprehensive blend of driving academic, industry, and government counsels, among them Riley Repko. As keynote speaker for SINET's October 27 and 28 occasion, previous Department of Homeland Security Secretary Michael Chertoff punctuated the massiveness and seriousness of the digital risk, saying among numerous essential messages, that "without security, we can't have protection."

We can accomplish a significant Return on Investment (ROI) from an offer every fight.

To meet the security requests of the 21st-century associations are progressively perceiving their interconnectivity and relationship with the extreme condition. The outer situation consistently makes requests and makes openings expecting organizations to comprehend and adjust in like manner. Any move made by an association likewise results in the possibility of changes inside the extreme condition.

Numerous components impact an association's level of defenselessness to security chance. There are the more common factors, for example, the business working model, business execution and the association's history and the inexorably persuasive outer specialists including clients, intrigue or weight gatherings, networks and the media that are all themselves powerless to impact. The social obligation profile of an association for instance regardless of whether real or saw can fundamentally build the possibility of dangers to the security of a business.

To give the profundity and expansiveness of security essential to ensure an association requires a security procedure that expands on existing work on, fusing a more significant amount of comprehension to set up why those issuing or completing a danger have taken the choice to do as such from the setting of their condition. Utilizing this data and working related to strong organizations it is conceivable to impact and co-deliver results that diminish or expel the risk.

The decision of those speaking to risk can be seen as the communication of three angles; the level of self-intrigue, enthusiastic decision and the social standards of the individual or gathering. The idea of the risk might be proactive, for example, an antagonistic organization in the quest for a particular goal or objective, or receptive as far as an office reacting to a business change or proposition.

Business Diplomacy offers a forward-looking, proactive system to connect individually or in a roundabout way with offices to determine, break down or redirect the risk.

Business Diplomacy spins around the recognizable proof of geopolitical and social factors that can influence an organization's tasks, both at home and abroad, and the expansive scope of legislative and non-administrative partners who can shape how those elements affect on the organization. It utilizes this investigation to help create systems of data and impact among the key partners. These systems are like this used to develop "alliances of the eager" to advance and ensure the organization's business advantages. The methods can likewise be utilized to confine or disturb threatening partners or alliances of partners plan on harming the organization.

On account of cybersecurity, a Business Diplomacy driven methodology would distinguish those people or gatherings who speak to danger or may design dispatch an assault against the organization and their inspiration. This procedure would be bolstered by insight, for example, the different information scratching innovations that permit internet checking of chatrooms, web-based life and different wellsprings of data about any potential digital assailant's aims. The investigation would likewise recognize those legislative and non-administrative partners who might be more steady of the organization. Contingent upon the result from the study, the organization, would create methodologies, for example, disturbance, separation, training or redirection, for instance:

A disturbance methodology would either expect to diminish the danger through the exchange, i.e., to disseminate or resolve the contention or it would look to undermine the limit of the digital aggressors to complete an assault

A methodology of segregation would center around the inspirations of the digital assailants. Working with to a great extent non-administrative partners who to some degree share the motivations of the eventual digital aggressors, however not their strategies, the organization would look to separate the digital assailants inside their very own locale, expanding weight on them from their associates not to assault the organization.

A training system whereby the organization would build up an open discretion methodology to produce a political and social condition in which an assault would have neither rhyme nor reason

At long last, a system of preoccupation would utilize the systems to persuade the digital assailants to occupy their consideration far from the organization. Redirection will probably turn into a noteworthy cybersecurity procedure for the 21st century with organizations effectively seeking after this with NGOs, e.g., BP and Greenpeace.

The selection of a more forward-looking methodology consolidating Business Diplomacy will empower associations to develop multi-dimensional, arranged connections and relieve security hazards that exist in an undeniably unpredictable business condition.

The 21st century holds numerous difficulties for both private and open part associations. The mix of multiplication of worldwide supply chains, expanded disturbance in the global condition and strain to change challenges even the most experienced organizations. Many existing associations are currently working universally or on account of new organizations are worldwide from the origin. The global condition speaks to specialists that are not inside the control of the association but instead may have an immediate or backhanded effect on choices, exercises and the general achievement of the business.

The multifaceted nature and danger of the digital space

We are sharing data about the digital space, yet neither on the critical scale nor speed required. We are not managing conventional armed forces despite what might be expected, but rather awry dangers of exceedingly talented and smart people or groups with the capacity to do enormous harm. A moderately little speculation and a modest number of individuals can perpetrate unending harm at lightning speed. No principles administer this common danger that crosses effectively from singular protection to country states without imperative. To address this, the U.S. government recognizes the tremendousness of this hazard by building up the digital risk as a different area notwithstanding land, ocean, air, and space.

The hazard is huge. Regardless of whether we by and by executing business over the Internet or not, digital hoodlums may deliver our restorative chronicles, void our financial balances, and demolish our FICO assessments. Our economies and necessary frameworks rely on the Internet. Sharp digital wizards can utilize any bit of innovation with an IP deliver to harm our basic foundation, thump out dams and influence frameworks, take cash from private and open budgetary establishments, wreak destruction with our supply chains, and, harm our PC systems. Digital hoodlums and country states have stolen many measures of protected innovation national safeguard mysteries.

Not understanding who, what, and where the most qualified assets exist before a digital danger happens looks at to "flipping through the business repository" to discover who can help us afterward.

Clashes between people in general and separate divisions are much more impossible to miss to the digital area. Citizens subsidize the administration's business to secure. Governments grapple with security, title experts, guidelines and arrangement issues. The private segment tries to turn a benefit and ensure upper hands, reacting to government's solicitations or surrendering, frequently thinking that it's difficult to manage government administration. The private part gripes that administration is unwilling to impart insight to industry, while the industry is unwilling to give to the government in light of worries about obligation and the conceivable presentation of restrictive data to contenders.

President Barack Obama and other government authorities have guaranteed industry officials that the organization's way to deal with Cybersecurity would be founded on motivations for collaboration as opposed to on control. However, some administrative specialist may be essential to get a compelling level of cooperation. At last, the private part will probably need to acknowledge some significant government control on Cybersecurity, setting up measures of training and baselines of security we can authorize.

Nobody is happy with existing conditions, and the ghost of the National Security Agency or the Cyber Command expecting control of the country's basic framework raises genuine worries about fundamental freedoms and protection.

The chance

We have shared hazard and shared weakness as people, networks, countries, and the world network. First off, numerous individuals value the requirement for worldwide organization among government and the private-segment and have made noteworthy strides toward that path. For the best-shared advantage, why not address the whole range of intricacy from a comprehensive and fair-minded viewpoint?

Why not expand on the precedents of inventive reasoning in the digital space? Making noteworthy open doors in the Cybersecurity space for the two sides, the Security Innovation Network (SINET) bolstered by the Department of Homeland Security Science and Technology Directorate, encourages consciousness of imaginative beginning period and developing development organizations. Driven by Chairman Robert Rodriguez, its controlling board of trustees incorporates a comprehensive blend of driving academic, industry, and government counsels, among them Riley Repko. As keynote speaker for SINET's October 27 and 28 occasion, previous Department of Homeland Security Secretary Michael Chertoff punctuated the massiveness and seriousness of the digital risk, saying among numerous essential messages, that "without security, we can't have protection."

We can accomplish noteworthy Return on Investment (ROI) from a standard methodology. Why not pool assets to battle this fight together rather than independently, consuming tremendous assets, and hazard coming up short? The digital area can fuel instruction, work creation, and commercial development unhindered by geographic limits. We can animate economies by decreasing the robbery and annihilation of money related resources, privileged state insights, restorative narratives, protected innovation, and different resources. We can, at last, give more secure intends to lead the matter of both general society and private segment.

A universal collective structure

Why not encourage worldwide organization through a nonpartisan and non-aggressive substance going about as a facilitator, clearinghouse or merchant? Wouldn't it be perfect to be able to use the experiences, attitudes, funding, essential foundation ability and arrangements from an extensive inventory of 'information hubs?' A sensible arrangement of administrative guidelines can characterize the rights and obligations of each side in an open private association. The own division has the lion's share of digital ability and offers the dangers, vulnerabilities, and obligations with the government. The unbiased substance builds up trust connections among parties, separates the necessary components into flexible plans, distinguishes specialists, and administers the whole arrangement. It can know ahead of time and connect with assets inside government, the scholarly world, private industry, and among business people. Digital abilities can be included, changed or moved by inclination or require, and arranged by each digital test. It can likewise recognize and actualize best practices from around the globe. This system can make new arrangements on the spot.

Individuals from the U.S. investment network are eager about this common condition, yet governments must help this similarly. As noted national security venture consultant, Pascal Levisohn has expressed, "Such a shared domain could give an exponential change in capacities to protect the individual, modern, and government data and frameworks everywhere throughout the world."

The path forward

For what reason wouldn't we be able to set up this unbiased clearing-house as a 5013C non-benefit? This new instrument would animate trust, reasonableness, and mindfulness, and offer us the vast potential to reinforce our digital ability and tasks in manners yet just envisioned. This fair system can unfathomably enhance the government's capacity to work with business visionaries, the scholarly community, and others inside the private area. This will empower us to distinguish existing mastery and innovation that we may never have thought about, making exponential upside potential for barrier and financial development that can produce new arrangements on the spot. General society and private areas can support the work required to plan the business and innovation models to influence everything to occur. Eventually, the 5013C will connect with and encourage the general population and private segments to make our lives more secure and more secure, ensure our basic foundation, help social protection, invigorate financial development, and male occupations. For what reason don't we think outside the box and submit resources toward this worldwide open door with this new and novel methodology?

CYBER WAR: HERE NOW OR HYPE?

By a few records, cyberwar is now happening. There has been week by week reports of US frameworks being hacked from Chinese digital locations. Chinese hacking goes from U.S. government frameworks to Google mail to the specific PC on which you read this part. The Stuxnet worm attacked and handicapped physical structures of Iran's atomic power program for some time. It is broadly accepted to be the shared work between the legislatures of the United States and Israel. There have even been infections inside the USAF ramble direction.

While upholding for the foundation of the new U.S. Digital Command Headquarters in Maryland, Senator Barbara Mikulski (D-Md) expressed, "We are at war, we are being assaulted, and we are being hacked."

Safeguard Secretary Robert Gates' has been broadly misquoted as saying that U.S. Outfitted Services will consider digital assaults as a demonstration of war. Tending to the Defense Information Technology Acquisition Summit, he stated, "Luckily, to this point digital assaults on our military systems have not cost any lives... At the point when precisely is a digital assault a demonstration of war?"

The reasonable ramifications are that there will, in the long run, be a level of cyberattack not yet met that will create a military reaction. At that point tending to The tenth IISS Asia Security Summit in Singapore on June 4, 2011, he explained somewhat advance with an inquiry, "What might comprise a demonstration of war in the digital world that would require some reaction, either in kind or dynamically?"

Reports of cyberwar appear to be all over the place. Is CyberWar occurring and would we say we are nearly outfitted military clash, therefore?

Hang on a moment...

The US State Department says that the probability of a cyberwar between the United States and China is insignificant and isn't as of now happening.

Christopher Painter, State Department Coordinator for Cyber Issues, was particularly asked on October 18, regardless of whether there is a plausibility that a substantial scale digital war could break out among China and the US, and what might cause such a conflict. Painter reacted that "our activity is to maintain a strategic distance from any digital clash... Individuals gab about digital war. I don't think we've truly observed it." He said that the dangers that do exist are overstated and the job needing to be done to cultivate comprehension and trust preferably to than to expect such clashes.

America's Cyber-Security Coordinator ("otherwise known as Cybersecurity Czar"), Howard Schmidt said straightforwardly to a Wired magazine questioner, "There is no CyberWar."

Why at that point, do we hear a relatively steady drumbeat about Cyber War? Jerry Brito and Tate Watkins, in the pages of Reason Magazine, guarantee it's about control - controlling the data world and maybe (once more) the average PC on which you are perusing this section. They "noticed that alerts from individuals from Congress and government authorities about online dangers unfailingly incorporate talk about war, fate, or calamity. In any case, the proof they offer unfailingly identifies with things like surveillance, wrongdoing, vandalism, or flooding sites with activity through disseminated disavowal of administration (DDoS) assaults." They proceed to take note of that there's little-checked proof that there's a genuine risk from such online conduct, but instead that discussion about critical results (and us losing the race to fight digital dangers) is an endeavor to construct and grow a "cybersecurity-mechanical complex."

Subsequently, billions of dollars are being channeled into associations and organizations to fight a danger that might generally be in the creative energies of those would benefit from citizen largesse.

To take the point further, Dr. Thomas Rid, from the Department of War Studies at King's College London, contends in the Journal of Strategic Studies that digital war isn't presently occurring and will never happen. To be characterized as Cyber War, Rid echoes Carl von Clausewitz in saying that an assault would need to be "a conceivably deadly, instrumental, and political demonstration of power directed through noxious code," however that the most noticeably awful we are seeing and will see is "damage, secret activities, and subversion." These demonstrations, he contends, don't comprise presentations of war - digital or something else.

So we're left with the question: Is there Cyber War? Or on the other hand is the term it just a symbolic articulation of digital assaults that will never ascend to the level of good war? Are the consistently raising talk and media reports only a method for increasing more power over free self-articulation, does it speak to a benevolent inclination toward securing the people - or would they say they are at the same time both?

The appropriate responses will enable us to decide whether we're carrying on a modern spine-chiller, or if countries are sufficiently protected with current levels of security and frameworks safe enough with current levels of repetition. It's insufficient to sit inertly by while billions of dollars are tossed at dream boogeymen, making an inevitable outcome by planning and filling digital ordnance. In any case, neither does it bode well to overlook a looming digital calamity, if such is not too far off.

Be Safe While Being Social Online

The appearance of the web has brought the world closer and made it feasible for you to cooperate with your groups of friend's ideal from your cell phone or PC. Also, online networking stages like Facebook, Twitter and so on have made it less demanding than at any other time to keep the general population who matter to you refreshed about the incident in your life. It is no big surprise at that point that nearly everybody has a nearness on these stages. In any case, while this is the positive side of the online social world, there is additionally another more negative side to the majority of this.

An ongoing review by Cybersecurity firm Norton by Symantec directed in 2017 demonstrates that online badgering is expanding in India, with 80% of the overviewed clients confessing to having experienced some type of it. Online badgering can show in numerous structures. We've recorded the absolute most normal manners by which you can be annoyed on the web and furthermore some methods by which you can secure yourself against these dangers:

Data fraud:

In case you're on Social Media, the odds are that you have individual data - like your photos, subtle elements of your instructive foundation, your connections - coasting around. This gives online fraudsters the chance to take this data and utilize it to submit cheats or unlawful acts. For instance, fraudsters acquire own points of interest like your Aadhaar card number or individual data like email ID and after that utilizations it to complete deceitful or unlawful exercises, landing you stuck in an unfortunate situation. Sounds terrifying? It is.

Digital Stalking:

Have you at any point investigated the Message Requests you get in your 'Other Folder' on Facebook? On the off chance that indeed, and particularly in case you're a lady, you would have unquestionably gotten irritating messages from outsiders. This is only an essential level of cyberstalking and has been known to raise effortlessly. Not simply outsiders, but rather there is an expanding number of instances of cyberstalking by associates, companions, and family too. Not exclusively would this be able to be exceptionally baffling and irritating, however, can likewise prompt a circumstance where it ends up threatening and startling. What's more, it can without much of a stretch transpire.

Media Liability:

The more significant part of us considers our Social Profiles the place from where we can express our suppositions. In any case, what happens when somebody takes something you posted, takes it outside the realm of relevance and distorts your perspective? It sounds safe. However, it can arrive you stuck in an unfortunate situation. For instance, if you make a digital broadcast/web journals and somebody hacks into it, takes control of it and puts out a substance that is defamatory, infringes on any protected innovation or results in an intrusion of a person's privileges of security then you can arrive in a bad position.

So how would you ensure yourself?

Some fundamental practices you can take after to avoid such circumstances are:

Set robust passwords and don't impart them to anybody.

Check the security settings of your social profile and ensure that you've empowered the environment that keeps detached individuals from survey your points of interest or downloading your pictures.

Never share excellent points of interest like your telephone number, address or email address on your social profile, and if you do, ensure that they are escaped general society.

Try not to connect with outsiders, regardless of how commonplace they appear.

Control yourself while posting using your social profiles.

Acknowledge asks for just from known clients.

While these measures will keep you secured to some degree, hostile to social components that need to cause mischief will dependably figure out how to do as such. On the off chance that you wind up in an awkward circumstance on the web, you should report the occurrence or the client who is causing inconvenience for you. You can likewise hold up a protest with the Cyber Cell if things escape hand. Our Individual Cyber Safe Insurance will guarantee that the financial misfortunes that you could bring about because of such an occasion get limited.

IT security as we probably are aware it is encountering an insurgency. The immense number of heritage frameworks are supplanted by capacity and transmission frameworks that are more intricate, versatile, remote, and even equipment autonomous. The war between information safeguards and information criminals has been depicted as a wait-and-see game. When the white caps counter one type of dark cap detrimental conduct, another vindictive shape raises its revolting head. In what manner can the playing field be tilted for the InfoSec warriors? The appropriate response lies in these developing advances of this current year. Equipment validation the insufficiencies of usernames and passwords are notable. A more secure type of validation is required. One strategy is to prepare validation into a client's equipment. Intel is moving toward that path with the Authenticate arrangement in its new, 6th era Core vPro processor. It can consolidate an assortment of equipment upgraded factors in the meantime to approve a client's personality. Equipment verification can be especially critical for the Internet of Things (IoT) where a system needs to guarantee that the thing endeavoring to access it is something that ought to approach it. Client conduct examination: Once somebody's username and secret word are endangered, whoever has them can waltz onto a system and take part in a wide range of malignant conduct. That conduct can trigger a warning to framework safeguards if they're utilizing client conduct examination (UBA). The innovation uses vast information investigation to recognize irregular manner by a client. Contrasting a client's present conduct with past conduct isn't the primary way UBA can realize a malignant on-screen character. It analyzes how somebody is carrying on compared with individuals with a similar administrator or same office. That can be a marker that the individual is accomplishing something they shouldn't do, or another person has assumed control over their record. What's more, UBA can be an essential apparatus for preparing representatives in better security rehearses. Early Warning Systems Early cautioning frameworks are still in their most initial stages, yet they are being made to diminish hacking in an inventive way. These frameworks depend on calculations that endeavor to recognize destinations and servers that will be hacked later on. This view isn't centered solely on framework shortcomings; instead, it incorporates an examination of essential qualities shared by frameworks most much of the time hacked. For instance, a site that is known to contain a lot of delicate budgetary information would be a more likely hacking focus than another site that provides just non-exclusive business data. Such frameworks are not intended to ensure all destinations, or even locales with particular kinds of security, which is a takeoff from exemplary cybersecurity approaches.

www.ingramcontent.com/pod-product-compliance
Lightning Source LLC
Chambersburg PA
CBHW031218050326
40689CB00009B/1374